Life at the Edge

Life at the Edge

Why Australians love the water

CONTS

Play
8—39

Live
40—73

The body's
ancient memory
Jock Serong
6

The same sea
Amy Liptrot
7

TEN

Breathe
74—115

Discover
116—149

So, why do we love water?
Dr Deborah Cracknell
150—151

Contributors
152—153

Image Credits
154—158

Acknowledgements
159

Left to right: Currimundi, Queensland; Caves Beach, New South Wales;
Rosebud, Victoria; Gold Coast, Queensland

The body's ancient memory

When I was six years old and swimming in the shallows at McCrae on Victoria's Mornington Peninsula, I had an epiphany. Young for an epiphany, you might think, but actually quite old for one this daft.

It occurred to me, there in the milky warm water of the bay under an endless January sun, that the reason people couldn't breathe underwater is that no one had tried doing it through their nose. My grandfather sat in a low-slung beach chair in the shallows only metres away, a terry-towelling hat on his head, sipping beer through his fine silver moustache with his hindquarters discreetly submerged. If a crocodile could own a tin esky and a pair of floral Jantzens, then he was crocodilian in his watchfulness. The boats bobbed at their moorings. The fringe on the beach umbrella fluttered. I exhaled completely, stuck my head underwater, clamped my mouth shut and took a deep breath through my nose.

I forget what the logic was: I only know the experiment ended with my grandfather abandoning his Melbourne Bitter and hauling me, shocked and spluttering, onto the sand. Did I think there were gills up there? Did I think I'd evolved differently? Imponderables. It's only now, no longer a curious child and not yet a vigilant grandfather, that I wonder if I was onto something.

We do not visit the water and return to the terrestrial realm, I am beginning to think. We do the opposite: when we go to the water we are engaged in an act of returning.

We were immersed before we were born, suspended in a private sea of amniotic fluid, the composition of which is remarkably close to seawater – a solution of salts and nutrients. At four to six weeks, human embryos have gill arches and a tail: the arches are absorbed into the structure of our jaw and the tail becomes our coccyx, but for a moment in gestational time we hark back to an aquatic ancestor.

As much as we part from our mothers at birth and perhaps spend our lives drawing back to them, so too we are cleaved from the sea at birth and experience mysterious longings for its touch. For some, the pull is so strong that it can alter the course of a lifetime. We might call it exercise, ascetic ritual or time with a beloved friend, but submerged beneath the rationales, we are responding to an ancient calling. We don't know why we go back to the water, but we do, over and over again.

The exquisitely sensitive membrane of our skin reads temperature, salinity and movement, feeding an avalanche of information to the brain. On land, we forget that our weight is driven vertically down through our legs and feet, and how this burden is alleviated when we swim. A new equilibrium is established around the thorax: longitudinal balance is plumbed by our heavy heads, our feet working as rudders. Our hands, reaching into the void, find lateral symmetry. All the while our lungs are maintaining buoyancy: breathe in and rise, exhale and sink.

Swimming, merely being immersed, is a retreat to a place. A place where our eyes have forgotten how to see, but the webs between our fingers remember something, *something*. We can hear effectively but in a different register. The hierarchy of the senses has been rearranged to provide both serenity and alertness, but this can only be borrowed time. Swimming returns us to humility because we are ill-evolved in water: even the strongest are eventually helpless.

A part of the humility lies in having to disrobe, to strip ourselves of the identifiers we use on land – class, creed, fashion – and expose our skin in a way that's vulnerable, that places the sensual above the sexual. In reminding us of our animal state, immersion makes us equals. The early morning swimming group in my small town includes a GP, a builder, a man of ninety-three and another who's wracked by multiple sclerosis. Their roles, their titles and their pleasures or sufferings are anonymised by the brief moments in which they are swimmers. From the car park, they are merely heads in the gloom of dawn. In the water, they are goggles, plastered hair and flashes of goose-bumped skin.

These days, four-fifths of Australians live within 50 kilometres of the coast. I'm fortunate to be one of them. As years pass, the sea has become my office and my chapel, my pub and my armchair. I imagine that when I'm gone, they'll toss my ashes there, and I wish them an offshore wind for the day. When I'm by the water, I see its vital importance to people for a set of reasons that are both intimate and universal. In the darkness of deep winter afternoons, our kids, everyone's kids, race out to the beach after school, materialising out of paths in the scrub. They change in the bushes and throw themselves into the freezing shore break, gasping and shrieking. They surf, jump off rocks, swim or stand in groups in the shallows, all black rubber and white teeth.

None of them could tell you who thought of it, who sent the text message that drew them all down there, because they *all* thought of it: in the dying hours of a school day, they all wanted to return. It's a ritual daily migration, a thing that makes no conscious sense. Yet, it makes perfect sense: we are evolved to keep returning.

Jock Serong

The same sea

I grew up on a farm next to cliffs on the west coast of a Scottish island. The geography of my childhood formed my psyche, and those edges and horizons, the meeting places of sea, land and sky, inform all of my writing.

The border between sea and land is not fixed; it is an ambiguous zone constantly changing with the tides and moon cycles. The ocean encroaches where it is given access, and sea levels rise due to climate change. Shorelines and coasts are porous, and it is impossible to say just where an ocean ends and a continent begins, although many – cartographers and lawyers – try. On the island where I am from, farmers and property holders are said to own the land down to the furthest extent of low tide. In other places, the high tide marks the bounds or extent of ownership. Other interpretations of the limit of land rights include as far as a stone can be thrown, or a horse can be waded, or a salmon net can be cast.

Coast dwellers have a relationship with the sea that extends further than most. They bear witness to the intertidal zone – the area between high and low waterlines. Twice a day, the ocean covers these fascinating places and they become alive and flowing with sea creatures. Seaweed that lay flat when exposed now stands tall and sways as the forest of the sea. Shellfish and anemones can transform and move once more. When the sea retreats, the intertidal zone is a place of stillness again, cleaned and accessible to us picking in rock pools and walking on the beach.

I am fascinated by seals. These creatures in many ways seem human with their soulful eyes and haunting cries, but in reality, they remain unknowable. We can only enter a very small proportion of each other's territories: seals can haul themselves up the rocks a little and humans can wade and swim in only the shallowest parts of the ocean. It is for this reason, and more, that there is so much folklore around seals, in particular the stories of 'selkies' who morph between human and seal form.

As a sea swimmer, I am given some access to liminal zones. I like the idea that when I lift my feet, I'm no longer on land but part of a body of water making up all the oceans of the world, one that moves, ebbing and flowing under and around me. Naked on the beach, I am a selkie slipped from its skin. Sea swimming allows me to transgress normal boundaries.

Heat haze, fog and water vapour make the boundary between sea and land indistinct, as do the limits of our eyesight and perception; the horizon line is not always as certain as we think. I have experienced multiple mirages – seeing an island on the horizon inverted, ships and lighthouses appearing to be upside down. This occurs when very specific atmospheric conditions create refractions of light.

We stand on the shore, look out towards the distance. The sea that lies before the horizon is called the offing – hence ships due to come into harbour are 'in the offing'. How far it is to the horizon depends on how high you are above sea level. If you place your eye right down to where the sea meets the beach, you can't see very far. I am 6 feet tall, so when I look out from sea level the horizon is nearly 5 kilometres away, but from the top of a 53-metre hill this could increase to 26 kilometres. Nothing is fixed or as simple as it seems.

The intricate pattern of waves, rock and seaweed reminds me of the lightning-bolt moment I had when I first understood the 'coastline paradox', which explains how it is impossible to accurately measure the length of a coastline. The smaller the scale used to measure, the longer it becomes: a coastline is fractal, breaking into even smaller inlets and cracks, promontories and bumps – from hundreds of kilometres to millimetres. This accounts for the vastly different estimates of the length of coastlines.

Margaret River, Western Australia

Humans try to claim dominion over the ocean – by measuring and building – but only succeed for a short time. The power of the ocean cannot be held back. Houses built close to the shoreline are on borrowed time. A tidal swimming pool is replenished with fresh water twice a day. An old pier allows visitors to walk on water. How long will our sea walls hold? How long will our coastal cities stand?

The poet of my home islands, George Mackay Brown, wrote: 'The essence of Orkney's magic is silence, loneliness and the deep marvellous rhythms of sea and land, darkness and light.' It is these same juxtapositions that I notice in Australia's coastline, and I realise that although we're half a globe away, we all sit beside the same sea.

Amy Liptrot

PLAY

Life at the Edge

Opening page: Yallingup, Western Australia
Previous spread: Fitzgerald River National Park, Western Australia
Above: Rottnest Island, Western Australia
Right: Eraring, New South Wales

14 Life at the Edge

Above: Flinders, Victoria
Right: Whitsunday Islands, Queensland

Life at the Edge

Previous spread: North Beach, Western Australia
Above: Sydney, New South Wales
Right: Cape Schanck, Victoria

Play 21

Left: Port Douglas, Queensland
Above: Brighton, Victoria

Life at the Edge

Above: Byron Bay, New South Wales
Right: Bondi, New South Wales
Following spread: Rottnest Island, Western Australia

Left and above: Dungog, New South Wales

Life at the Edge

Above: Bunbury, Western Australia
Right: Black Rock, Victoria

Mornington, Victoria

Previous spread: Byron Bay, New South Wales
Above: Watermans Bay, Western Australia
Right: Scarborough, Western Australia

Play

Ramsgate Beach, New South Wales

Play

Above: Watermans Bay, Western Australia
Right: Gold Coast, Queensland

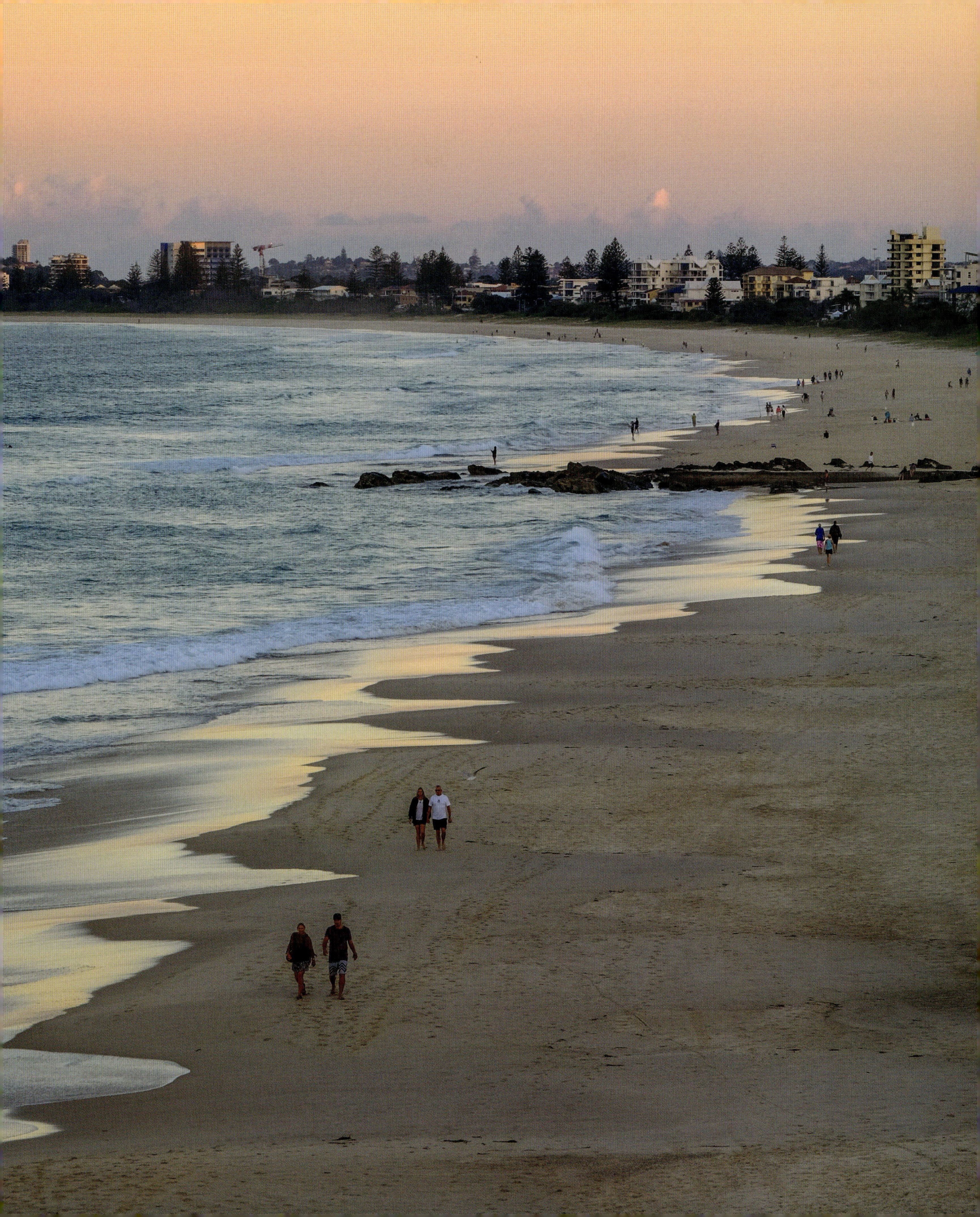

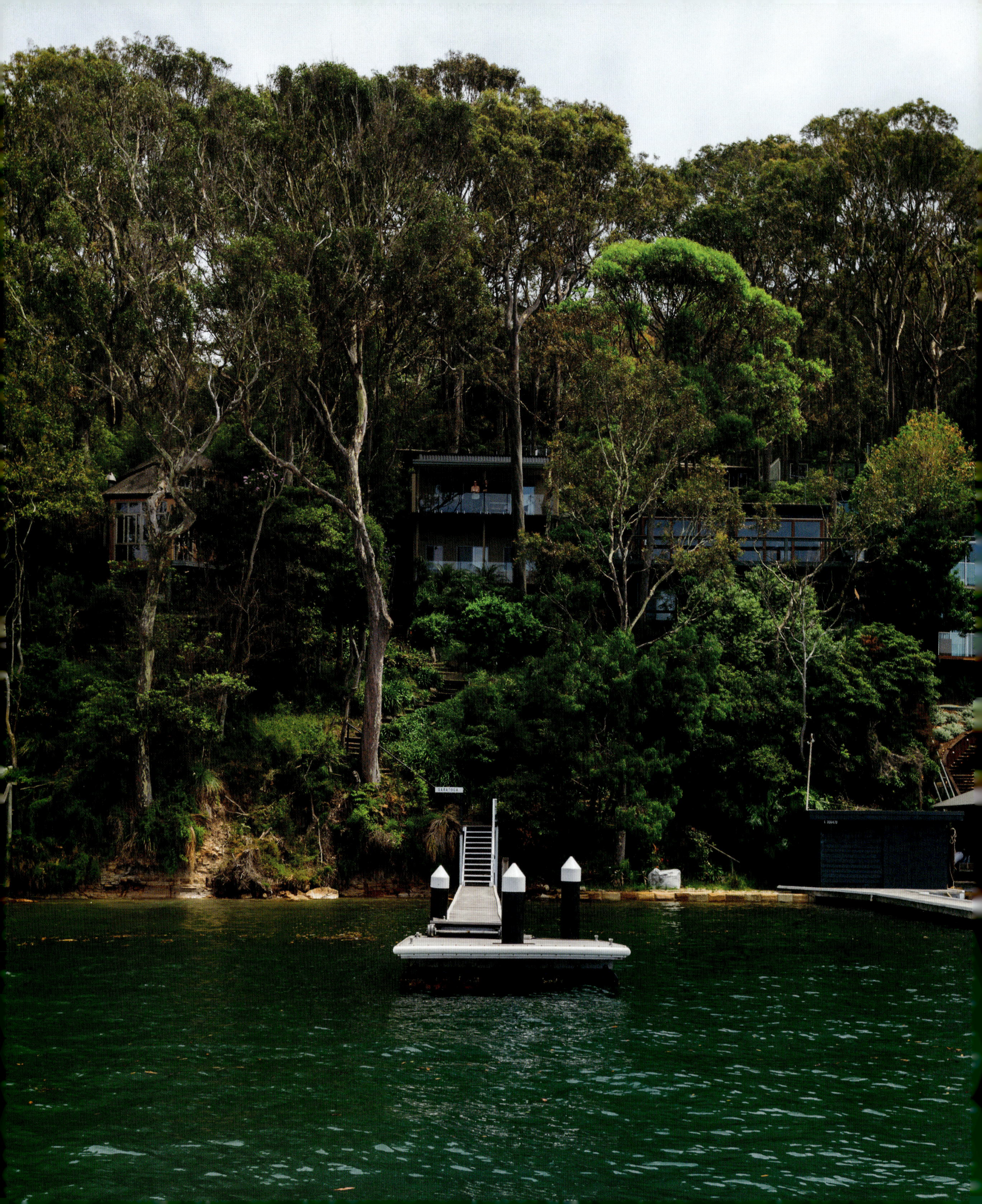

LIVE

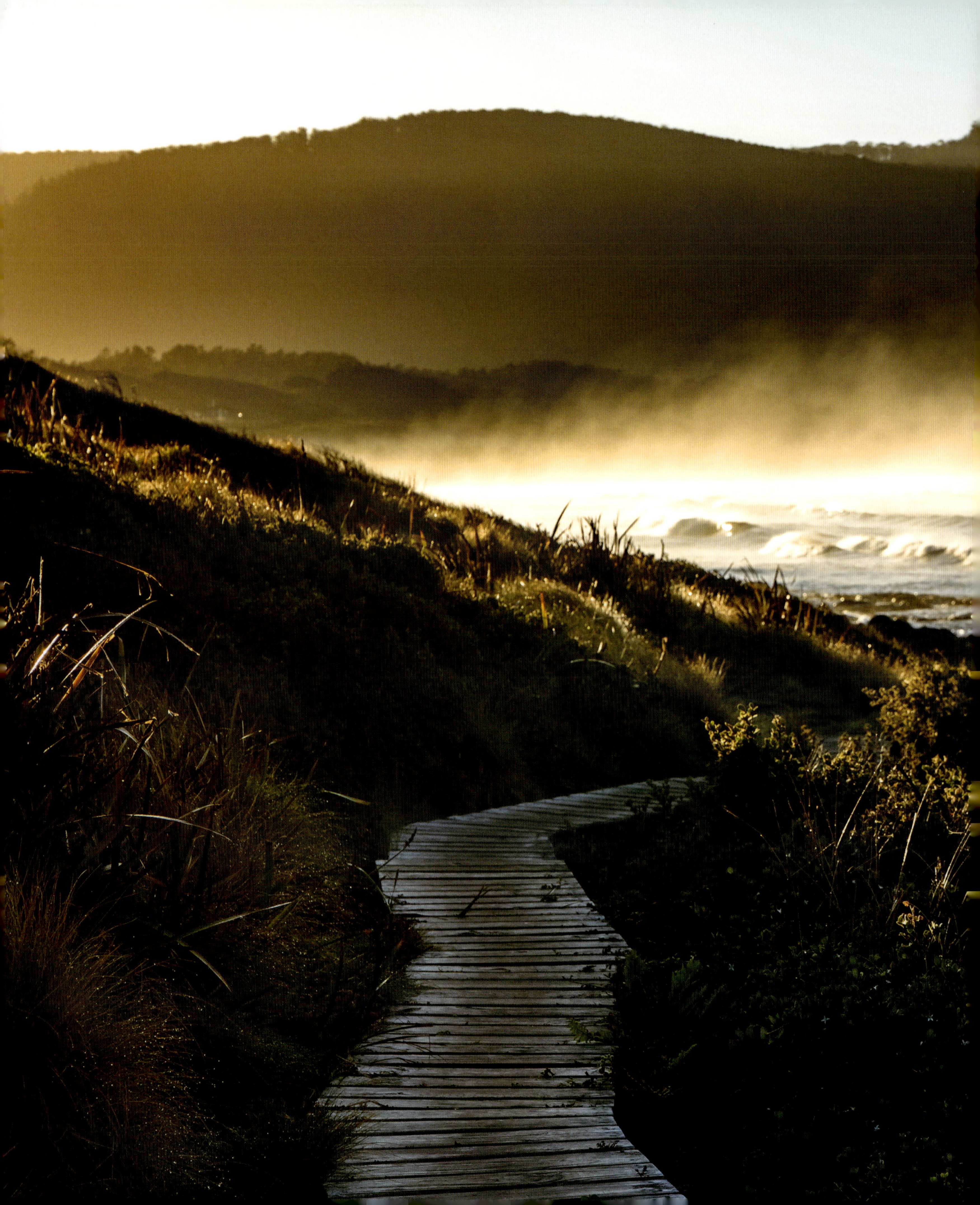

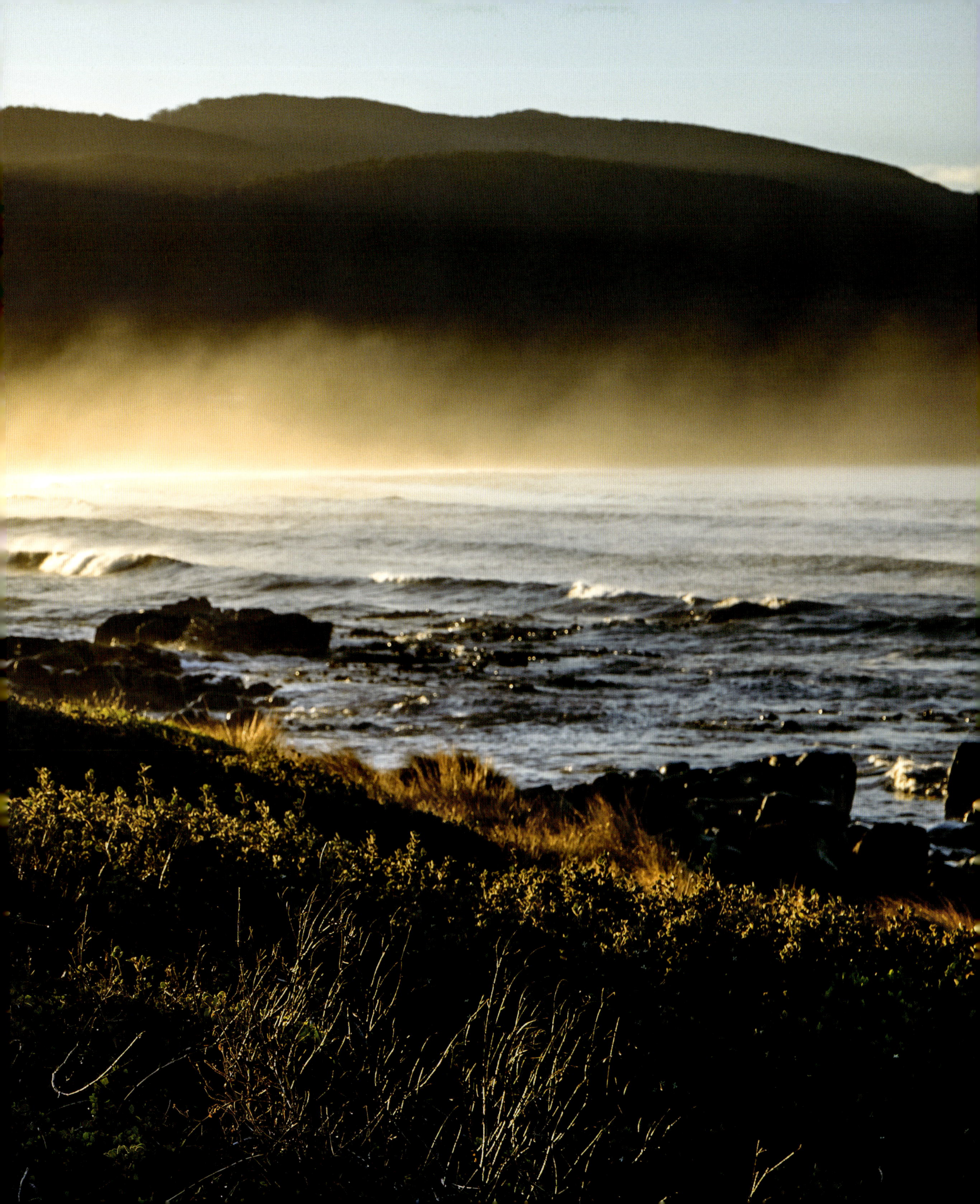

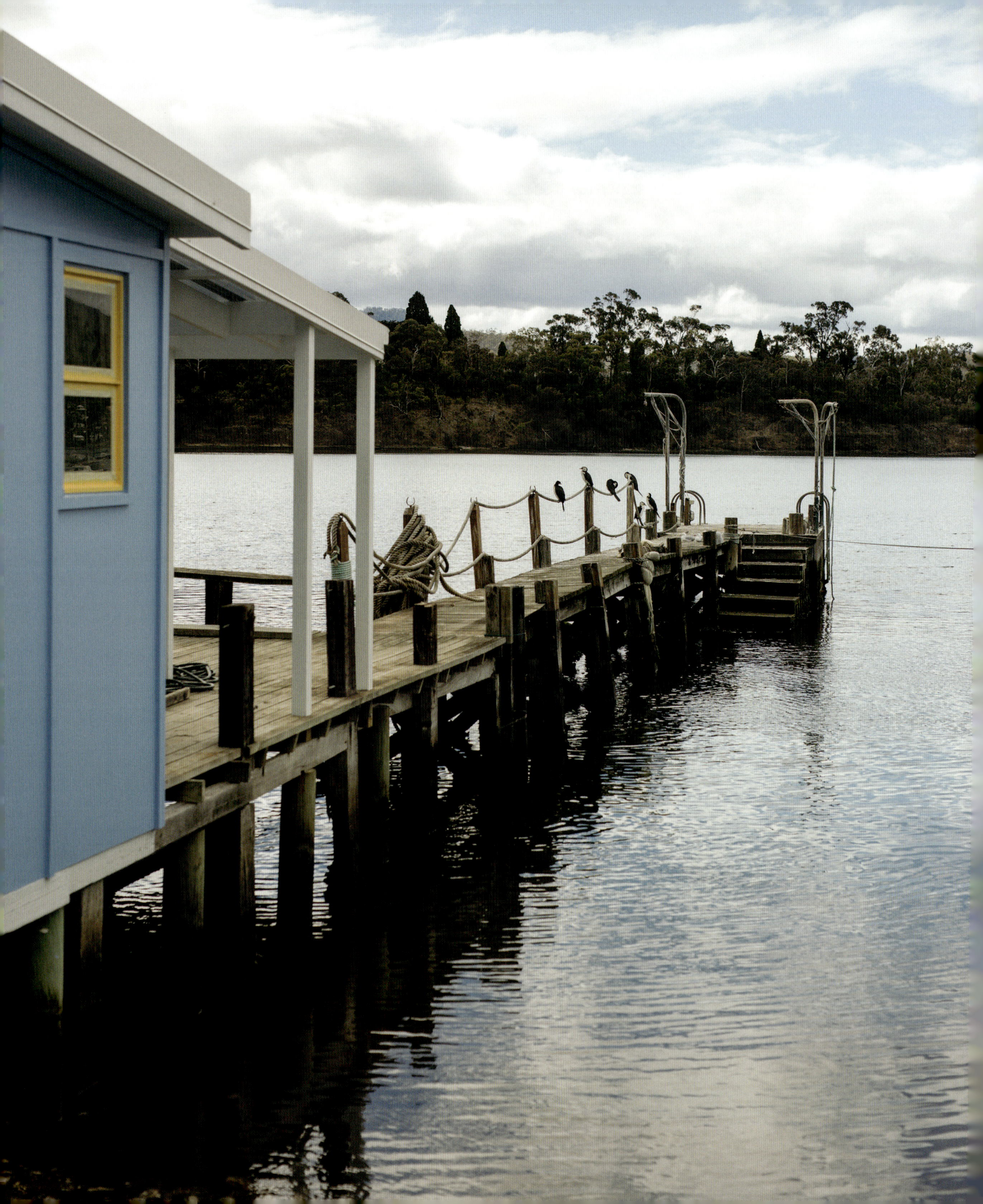

Live 45

Opening page: Pittwater, New South Wales
Previous spread: Bruny Island, Tasmania
Left: Cornelian Bay, Tasmania
Above, left to right: Swan Bay, Victoria; Pebbly Beach, New South Wales

Life at the Edge

Above: North Coast, New South Wales
Right: Gold Coast, Queensland

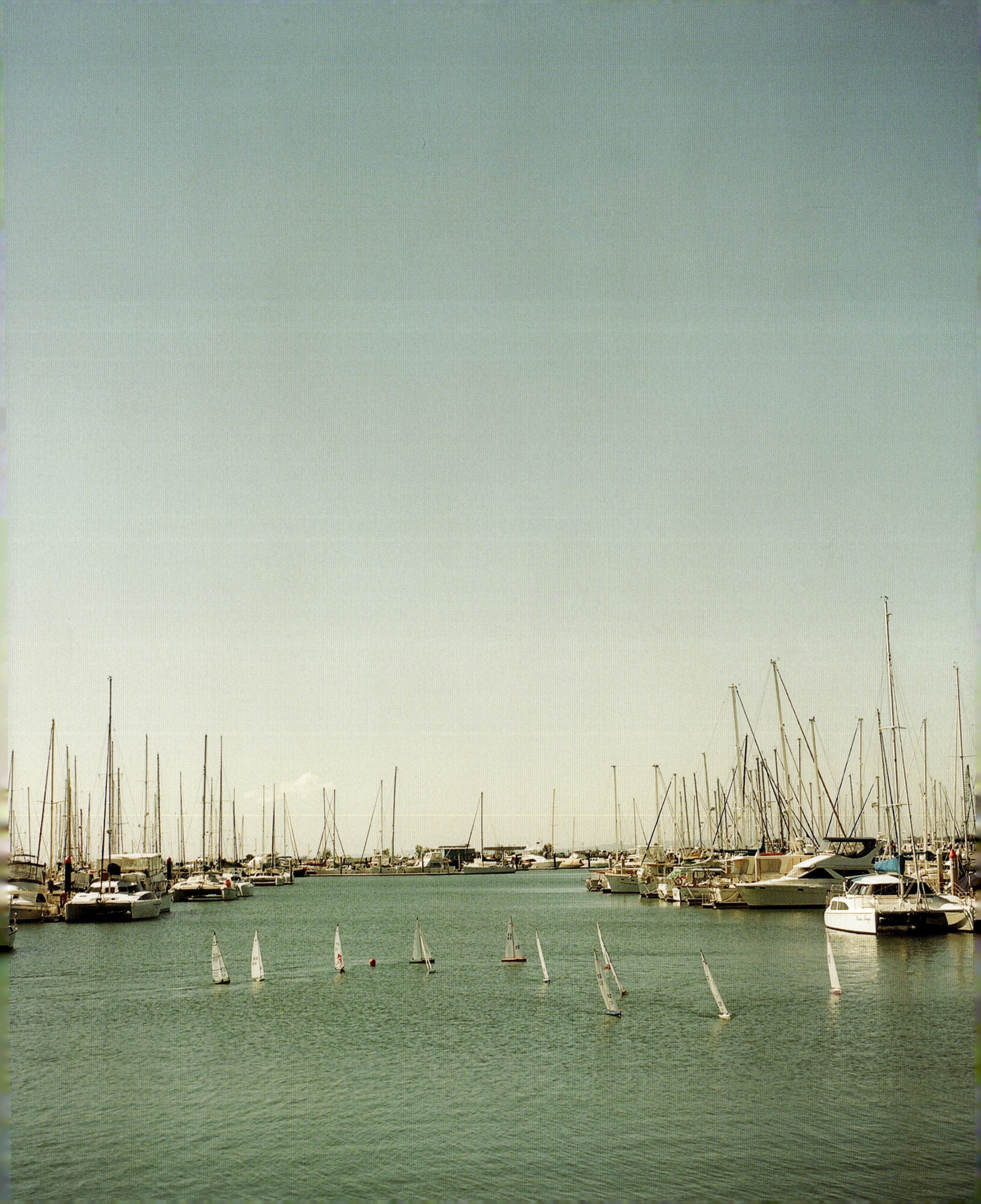

Above: Seal Rocks, New South Wales
Right: Perth, Western Australia

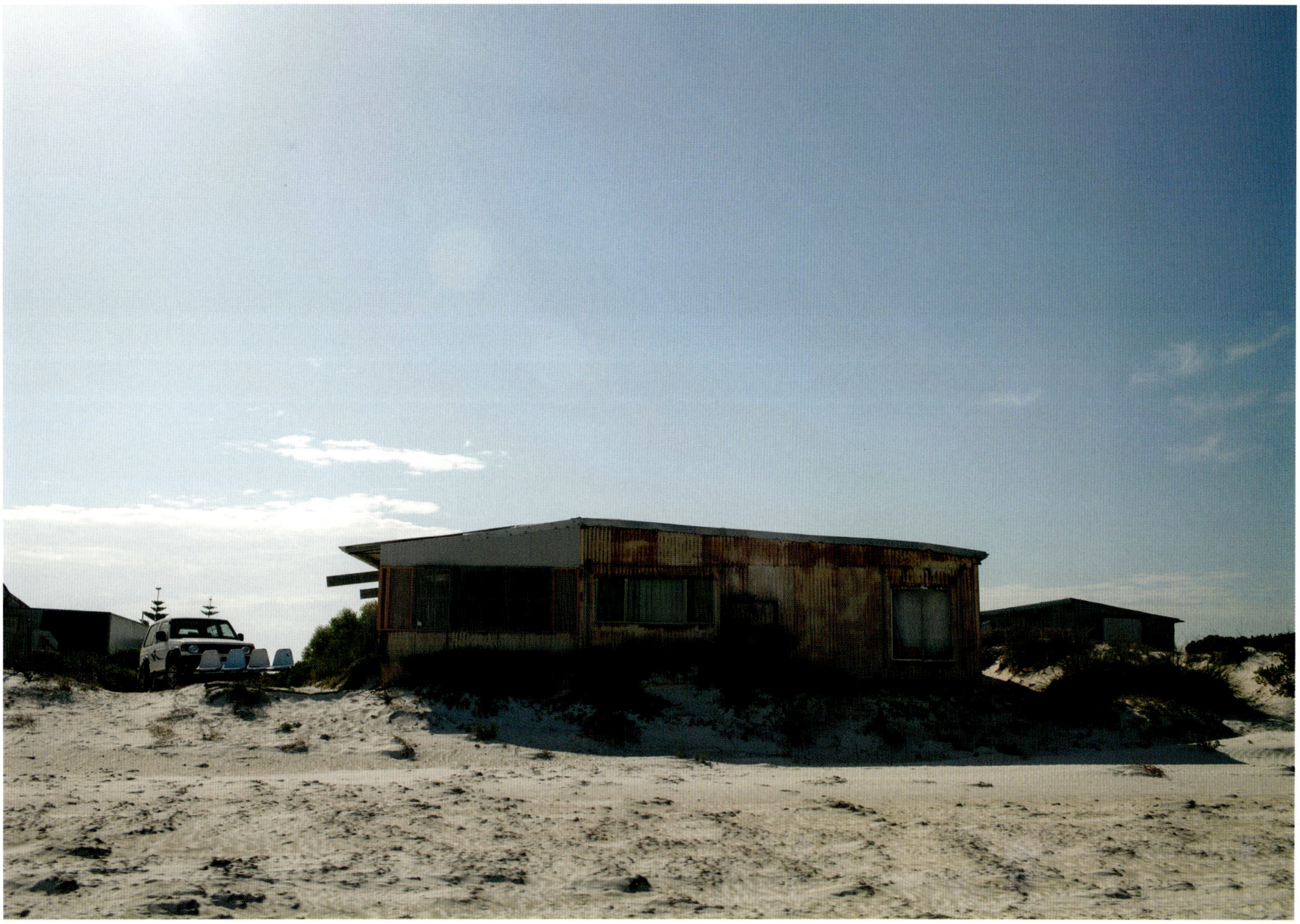

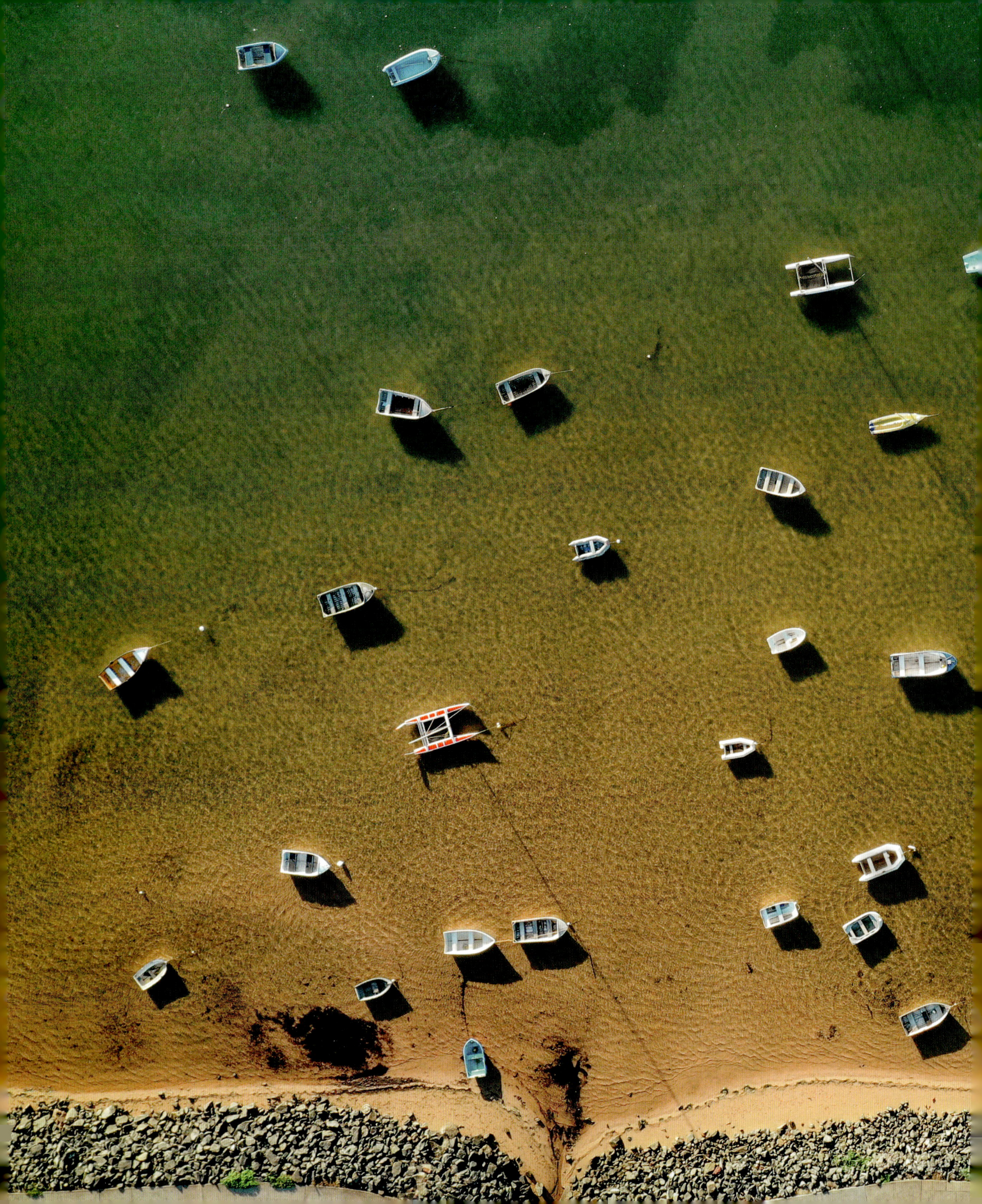

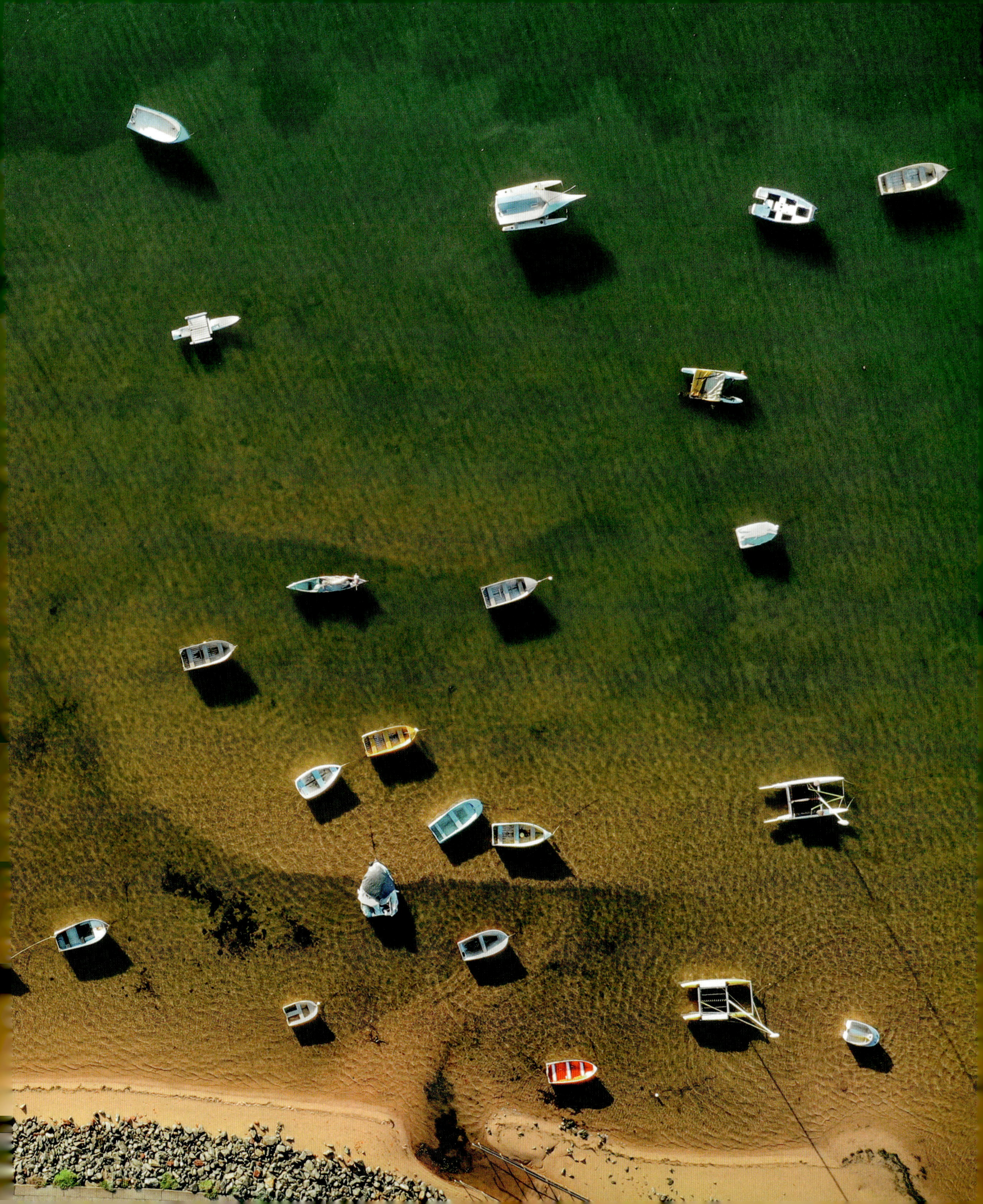

Previous spread: Victoria Point, Queensland
Above: Coalcliff, New South Wales

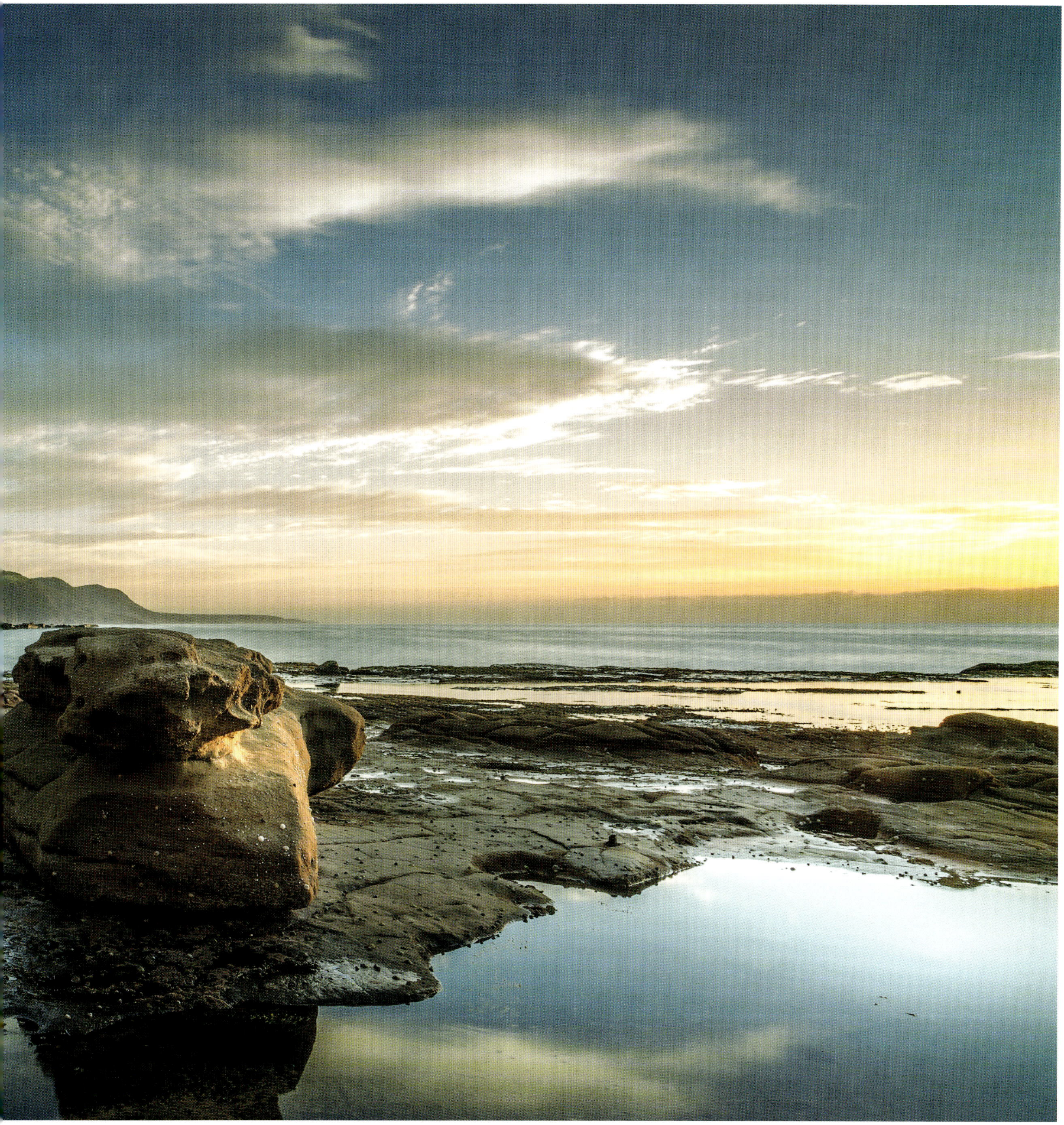

Life at the Edge

Left to right: Coolangatta, Queensland; Keswick Island, Queensland; Albany, Western Australia

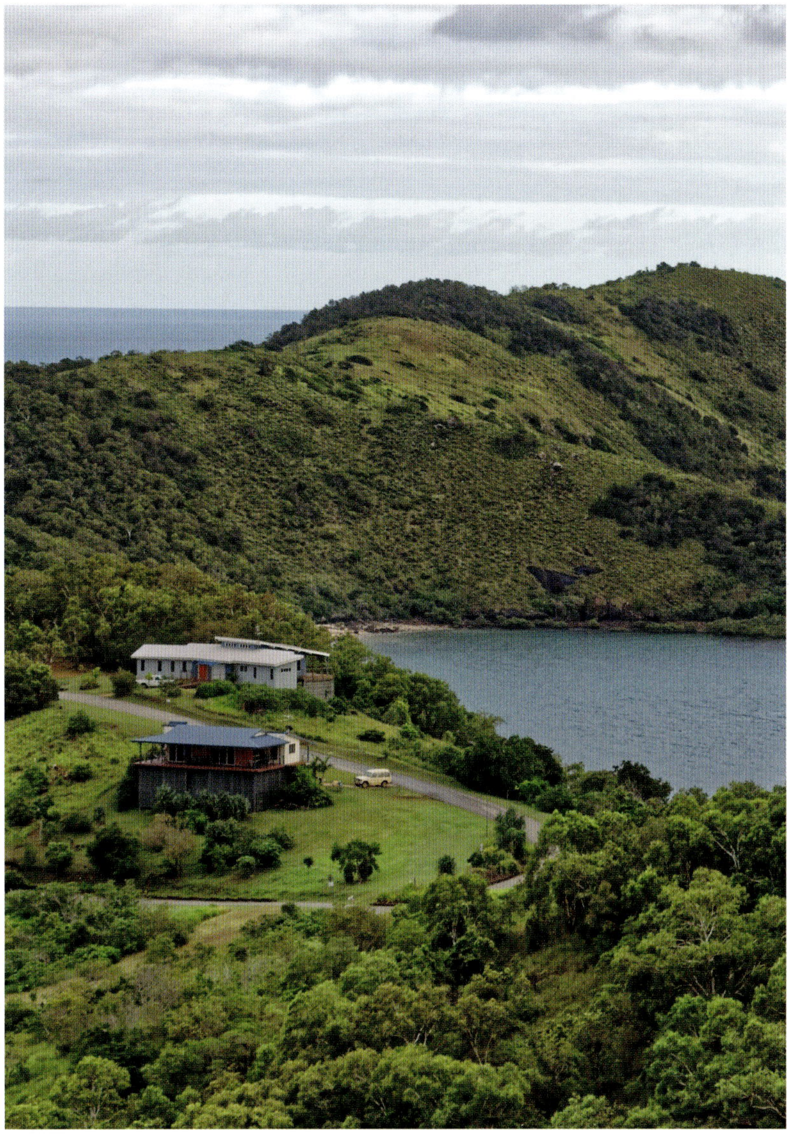

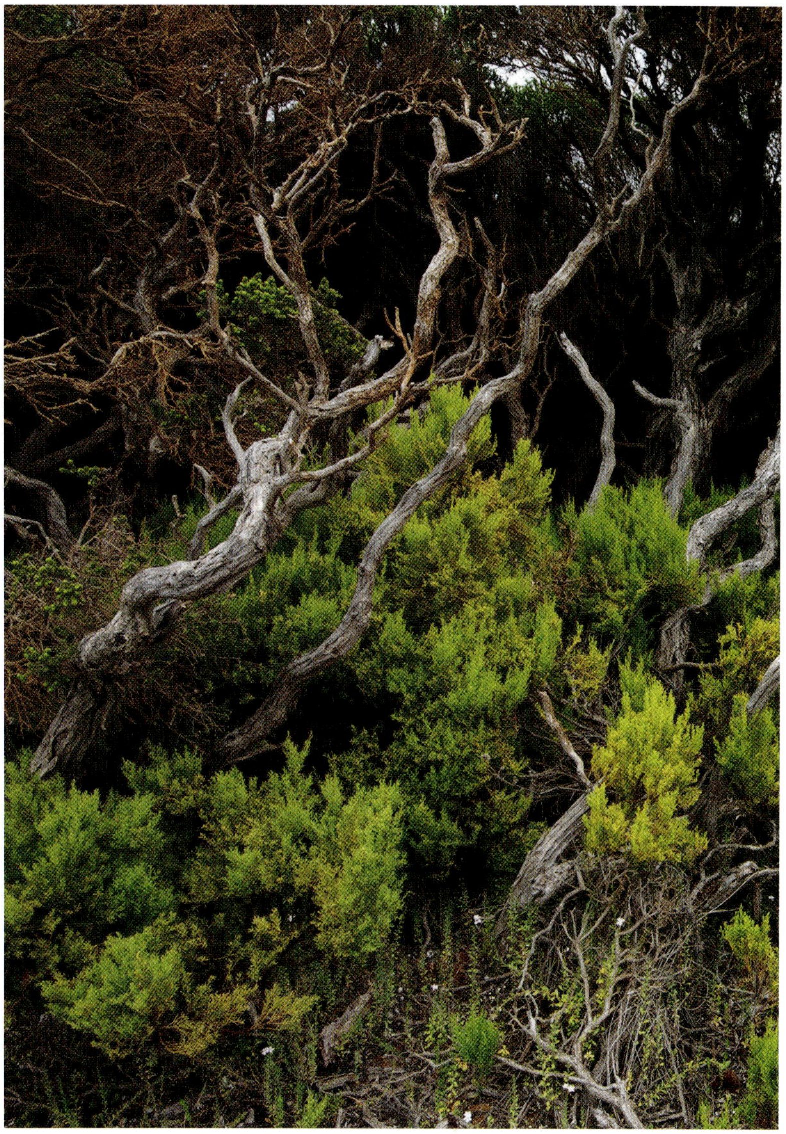

Above: Sydney, New South Wales
Right: Point Lonsdale, Victoria

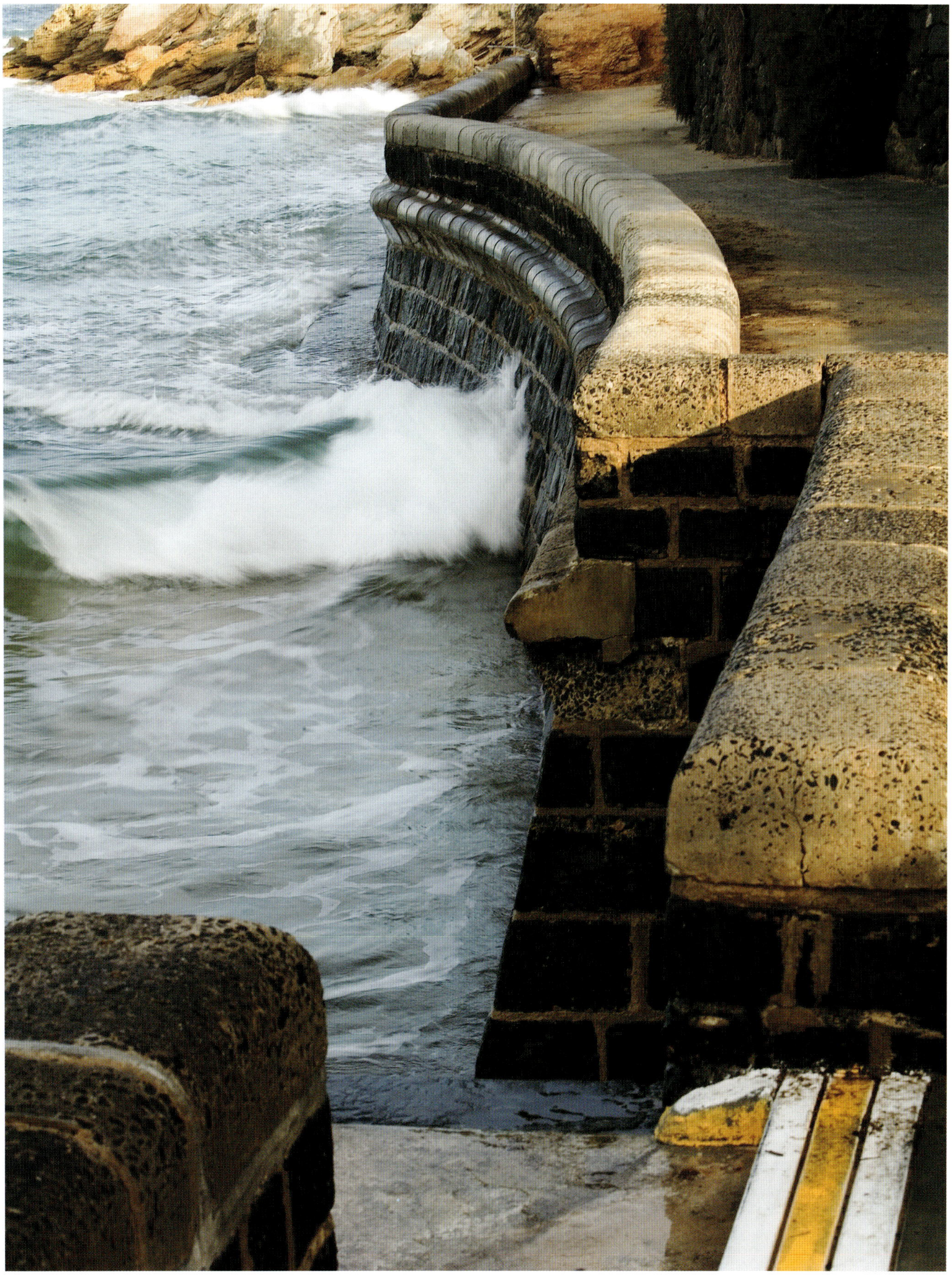

Life at the Edge

Left to right: Currimundi, Queensland; North Stradbroke Island, Queensland; Queenscliff, Victoria; Marengo, Victoria

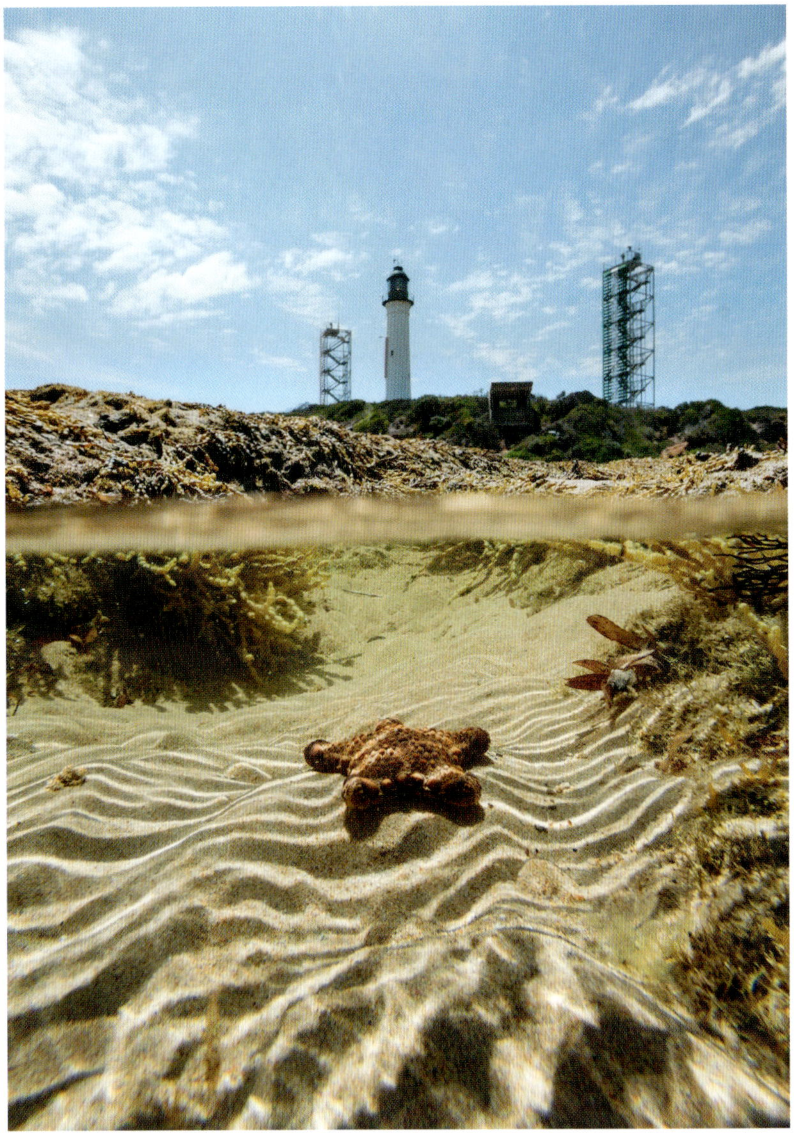

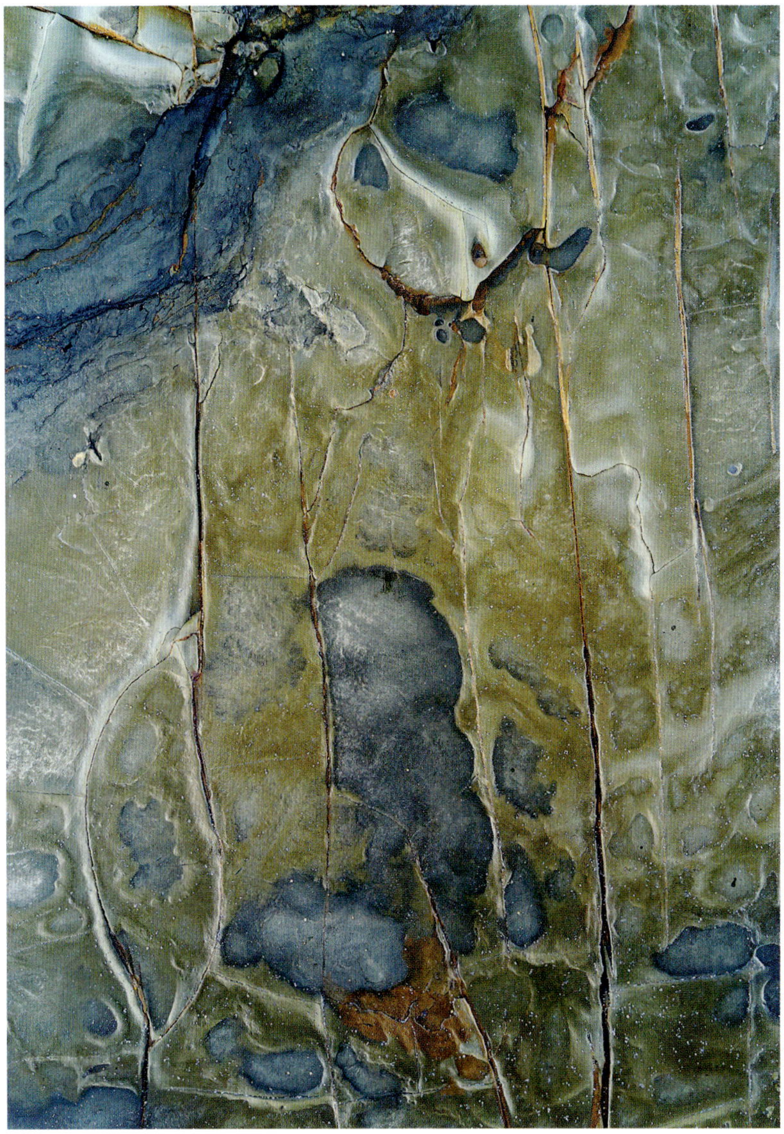

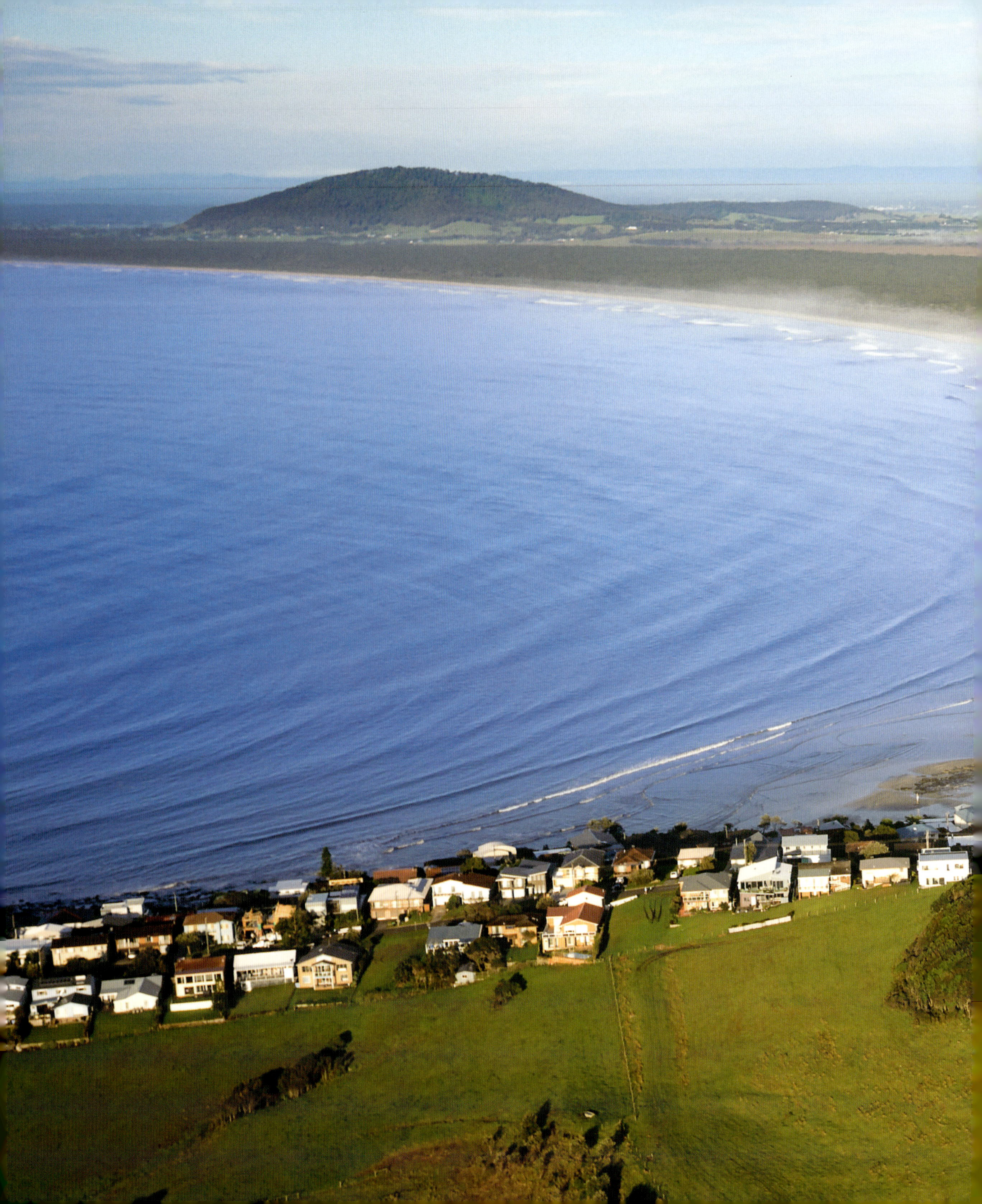

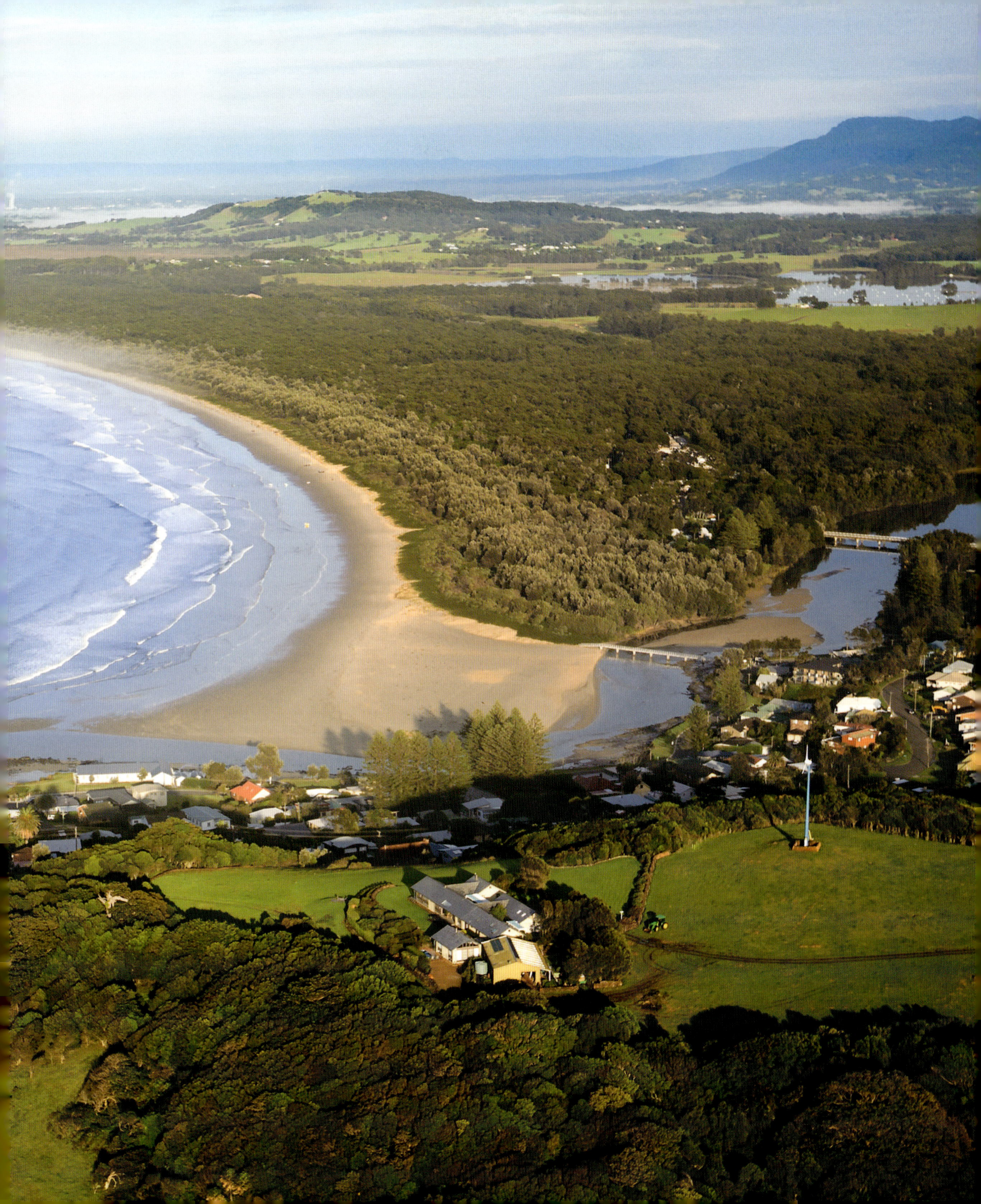

Previous spread: Gerroa, New South Wales
Above, left to right: Ballarat, Victoria; Aireys Inlet, Victoria;
Coolangatta, Queensland

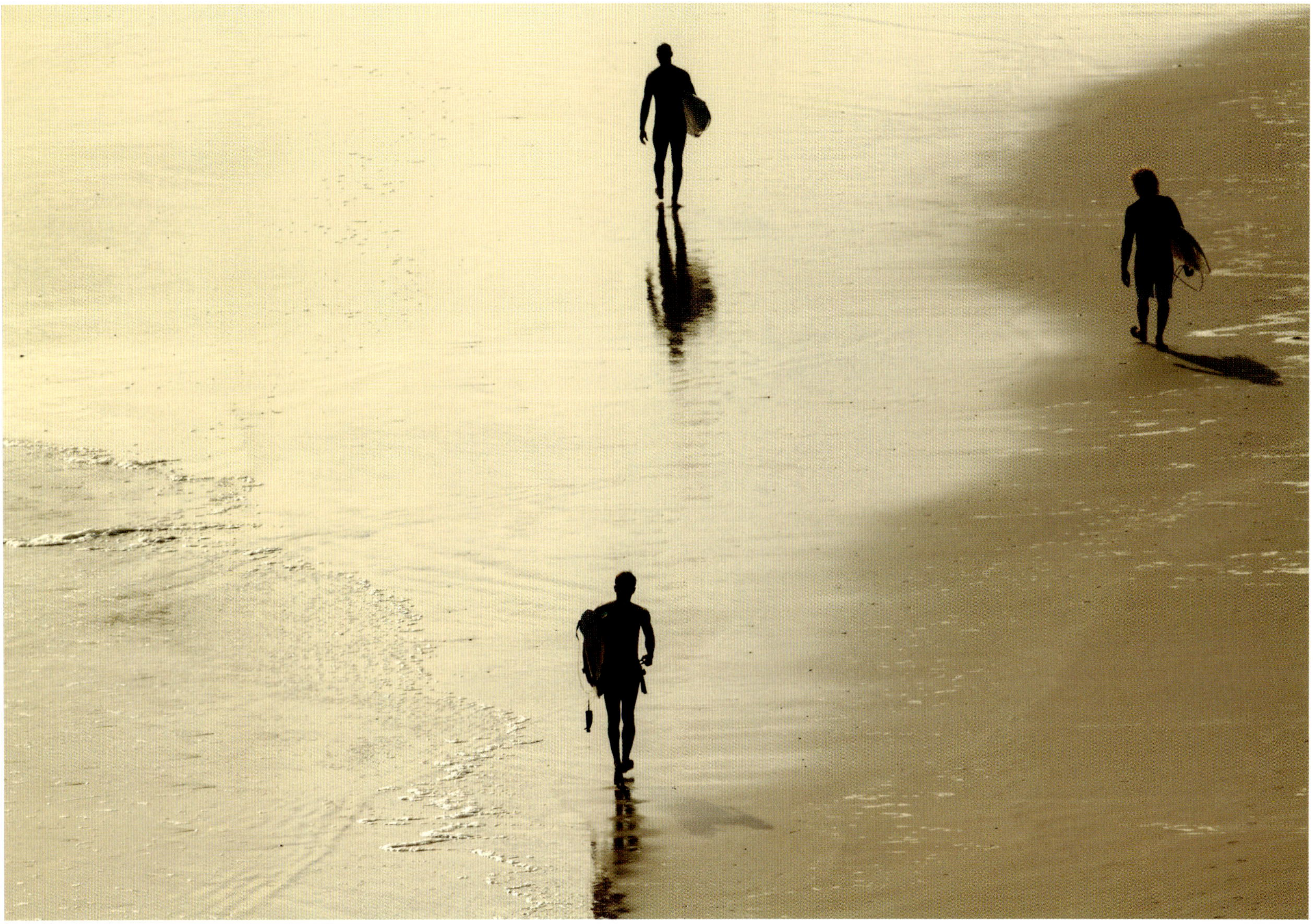

Life at the Edge

Above: Sherbrooke, Victoria
Right: Nelson, Victoria

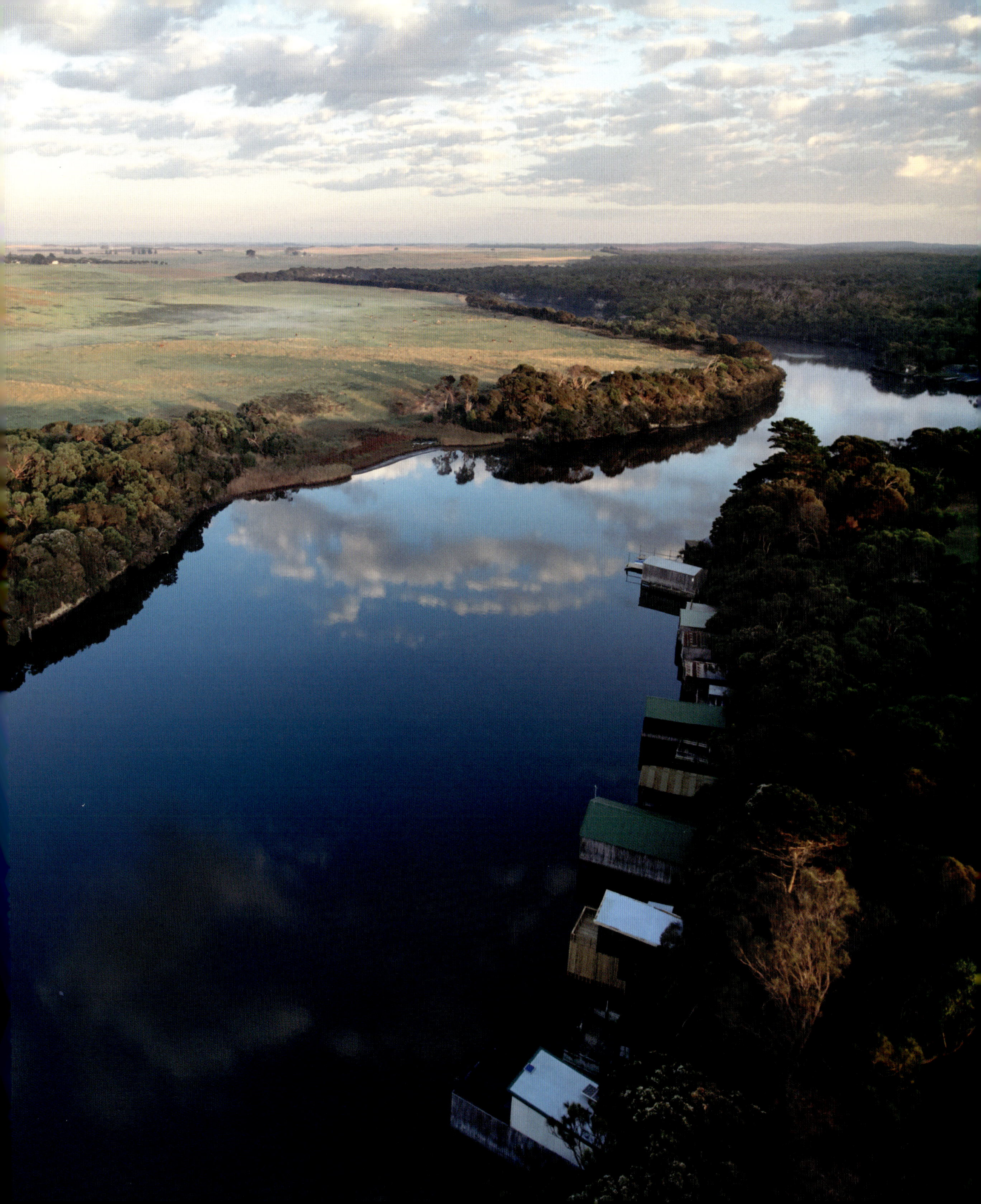

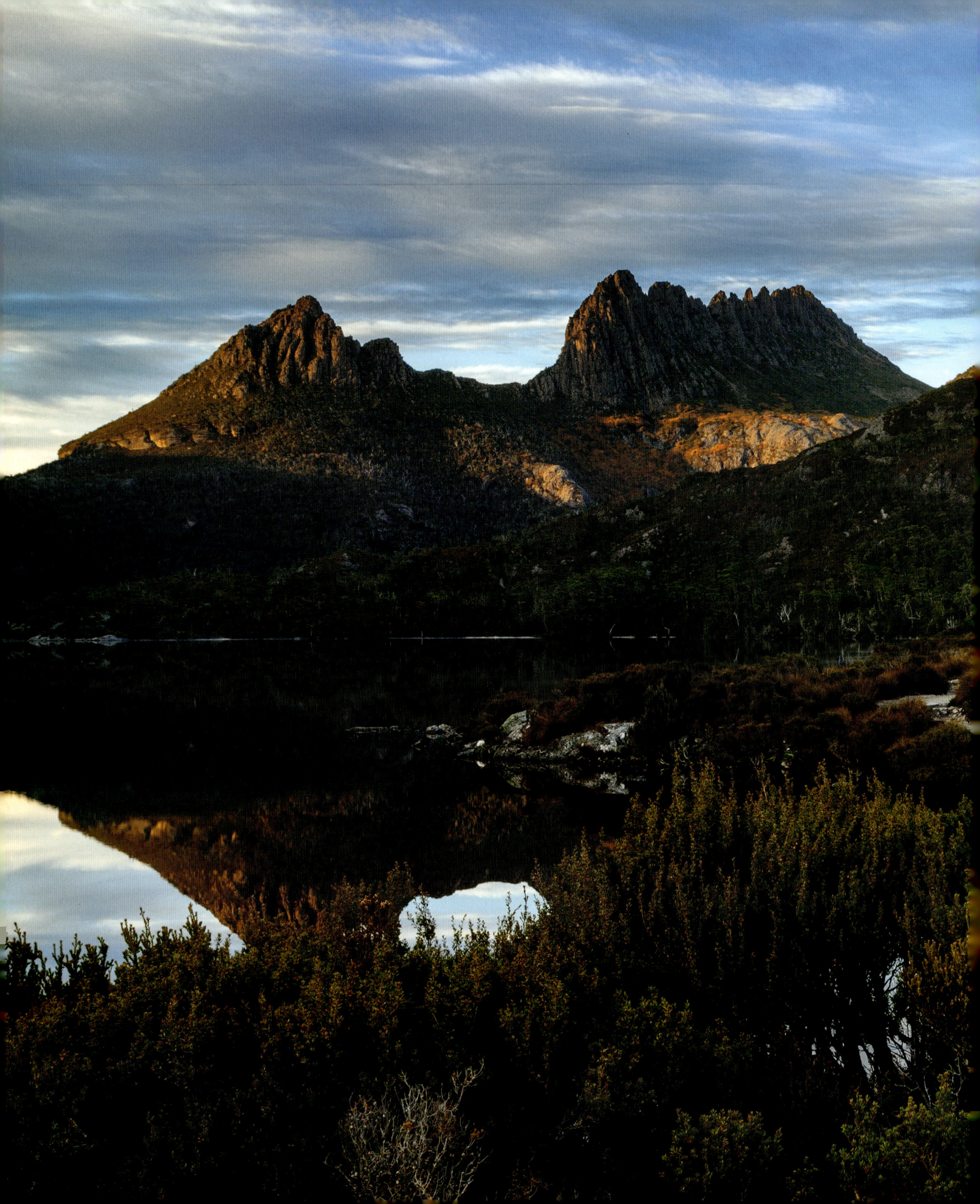

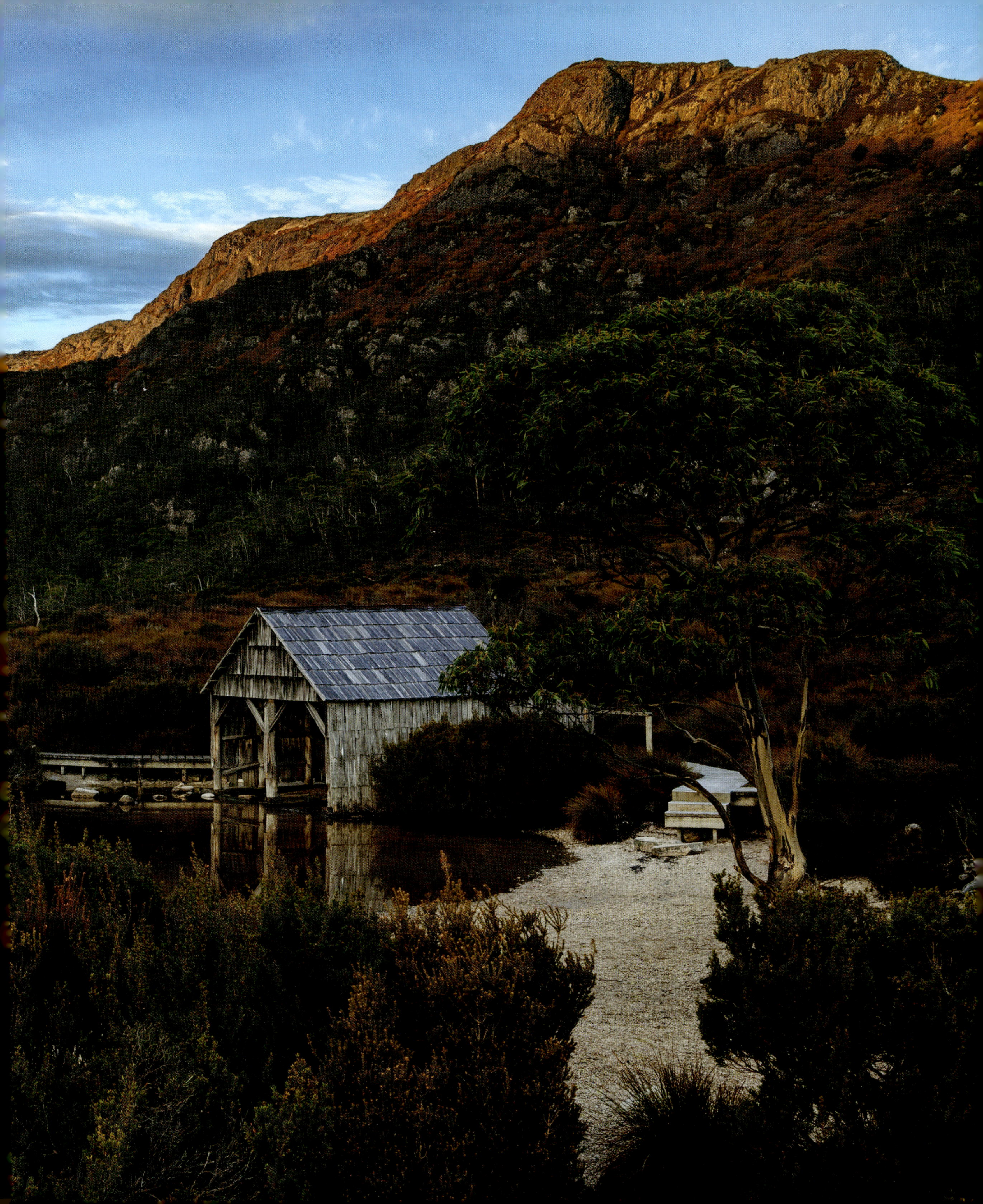

Previous spread: Cradle Mountain, Tasmania
Above: Buronga, New South Wales

Live

Life at the Edge

Above: Byron Bay, New South Wales
Right: Strathgordon, Tasmania
Following spread: Newcastle, New South Wales

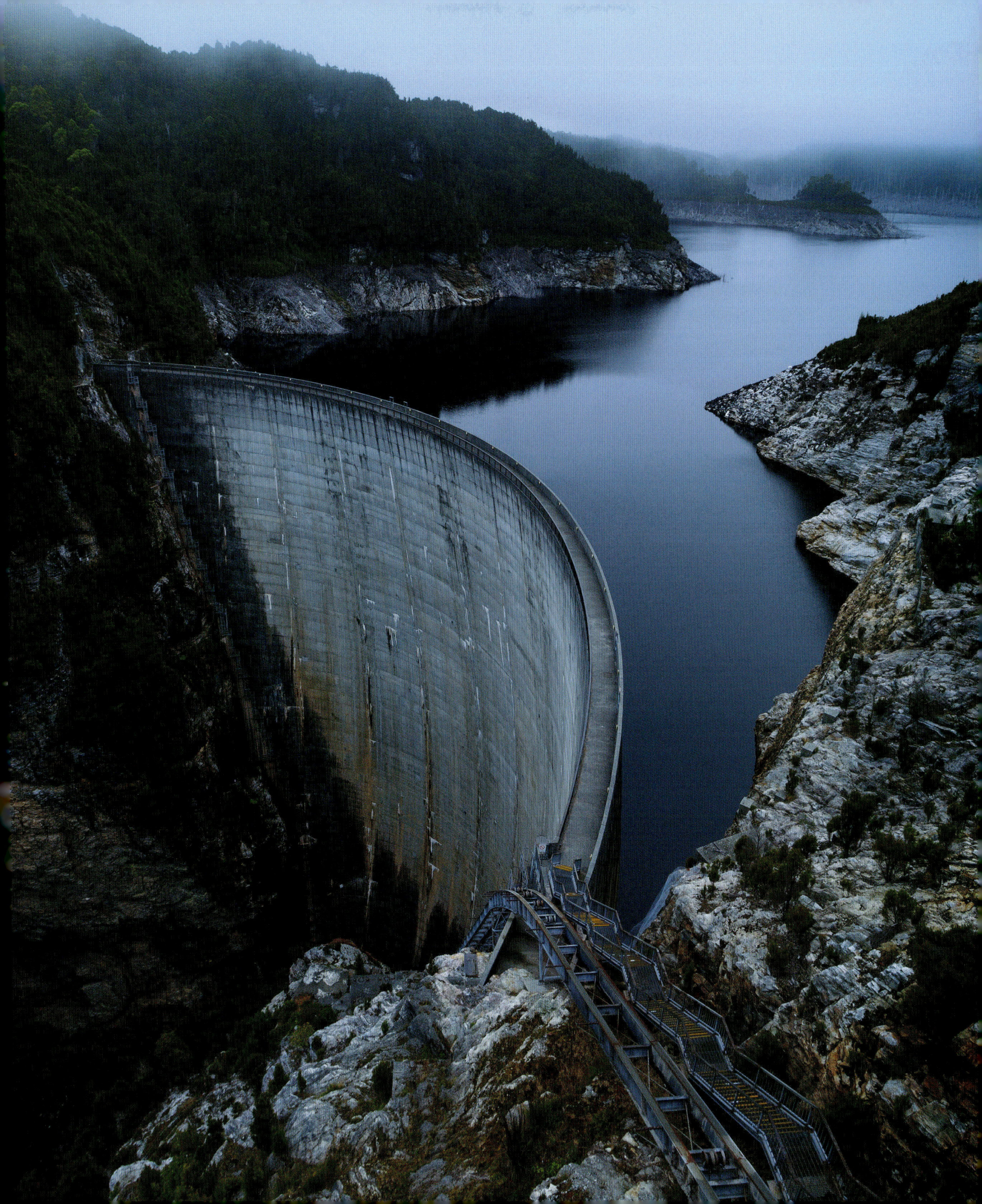

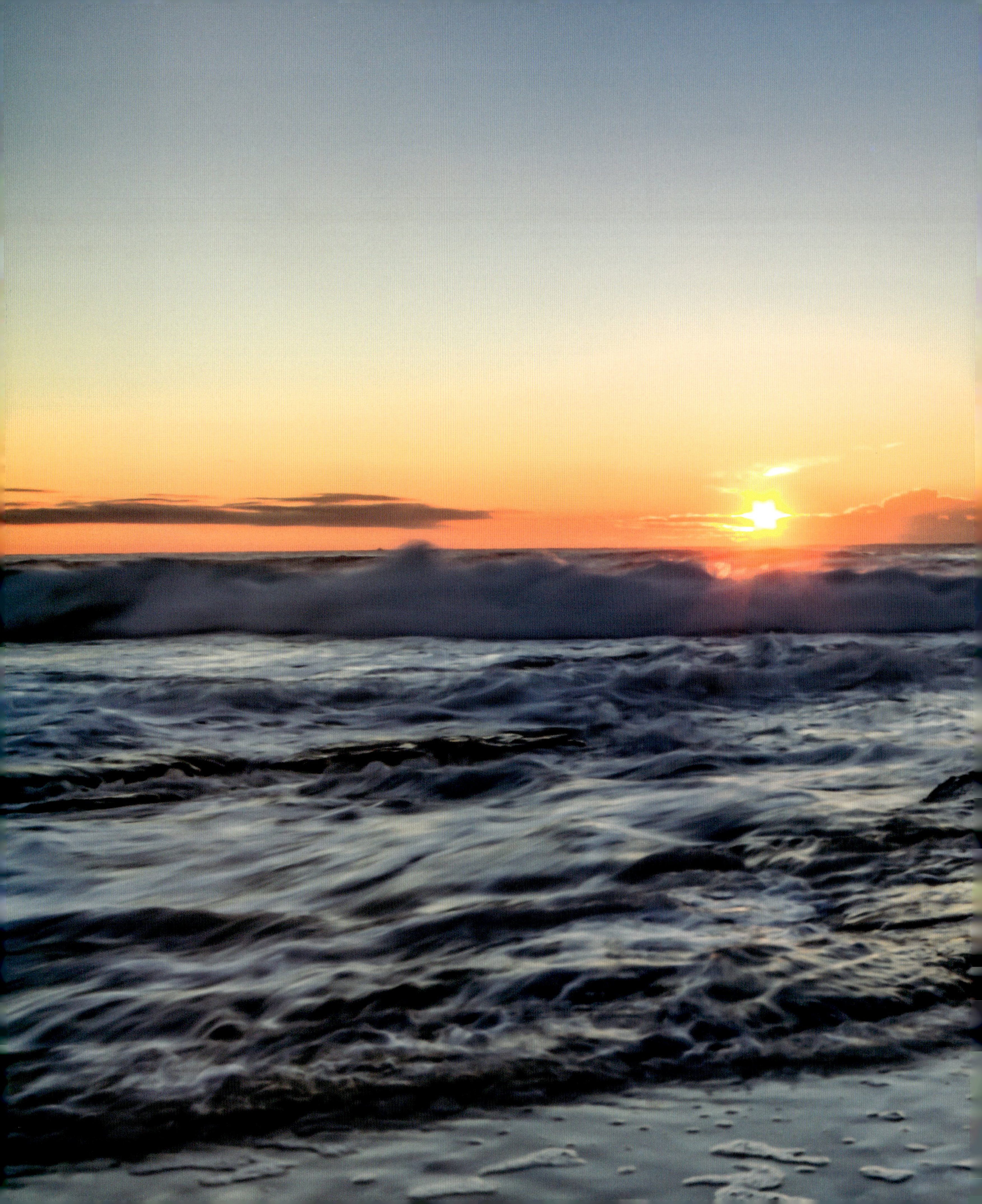

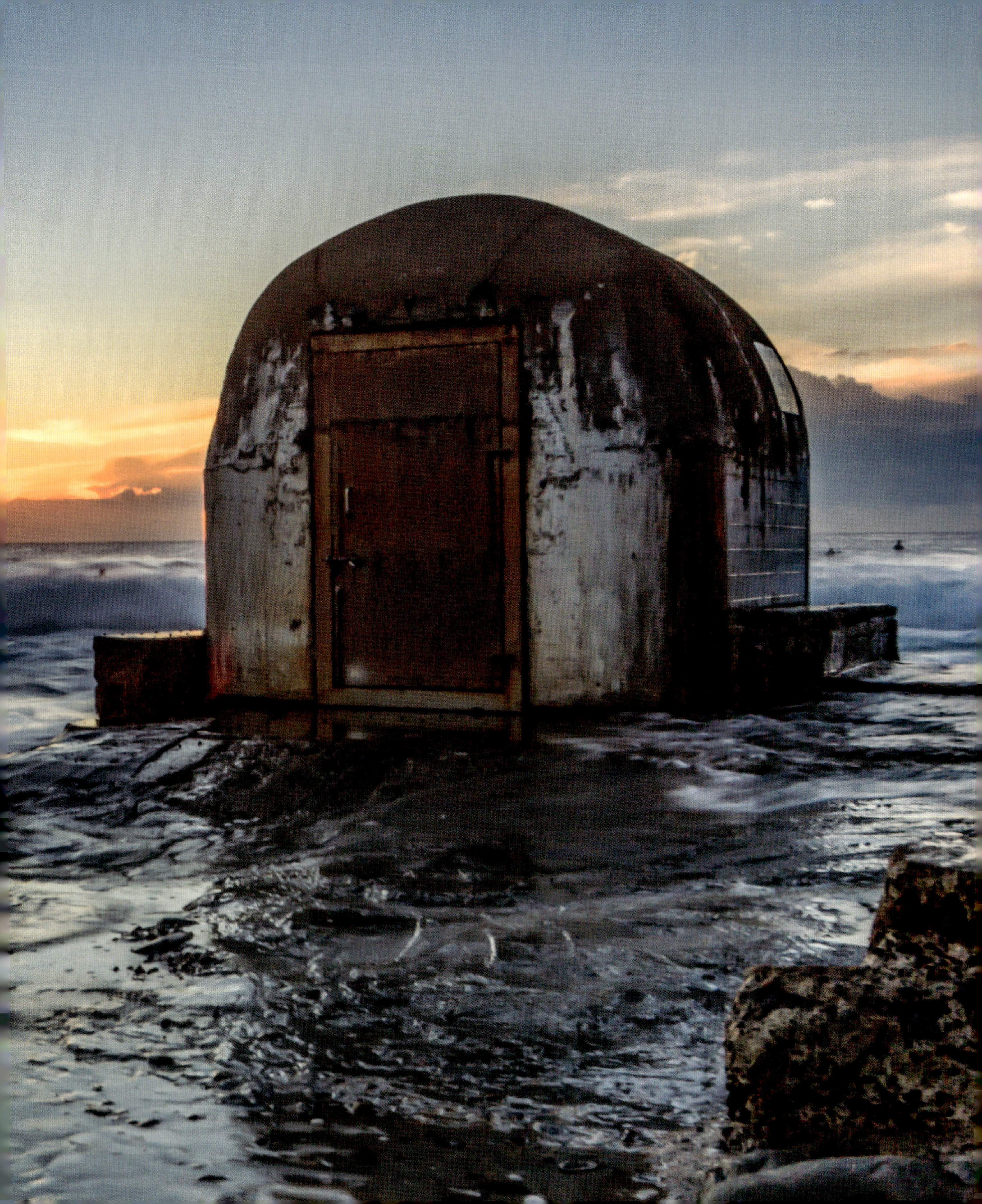

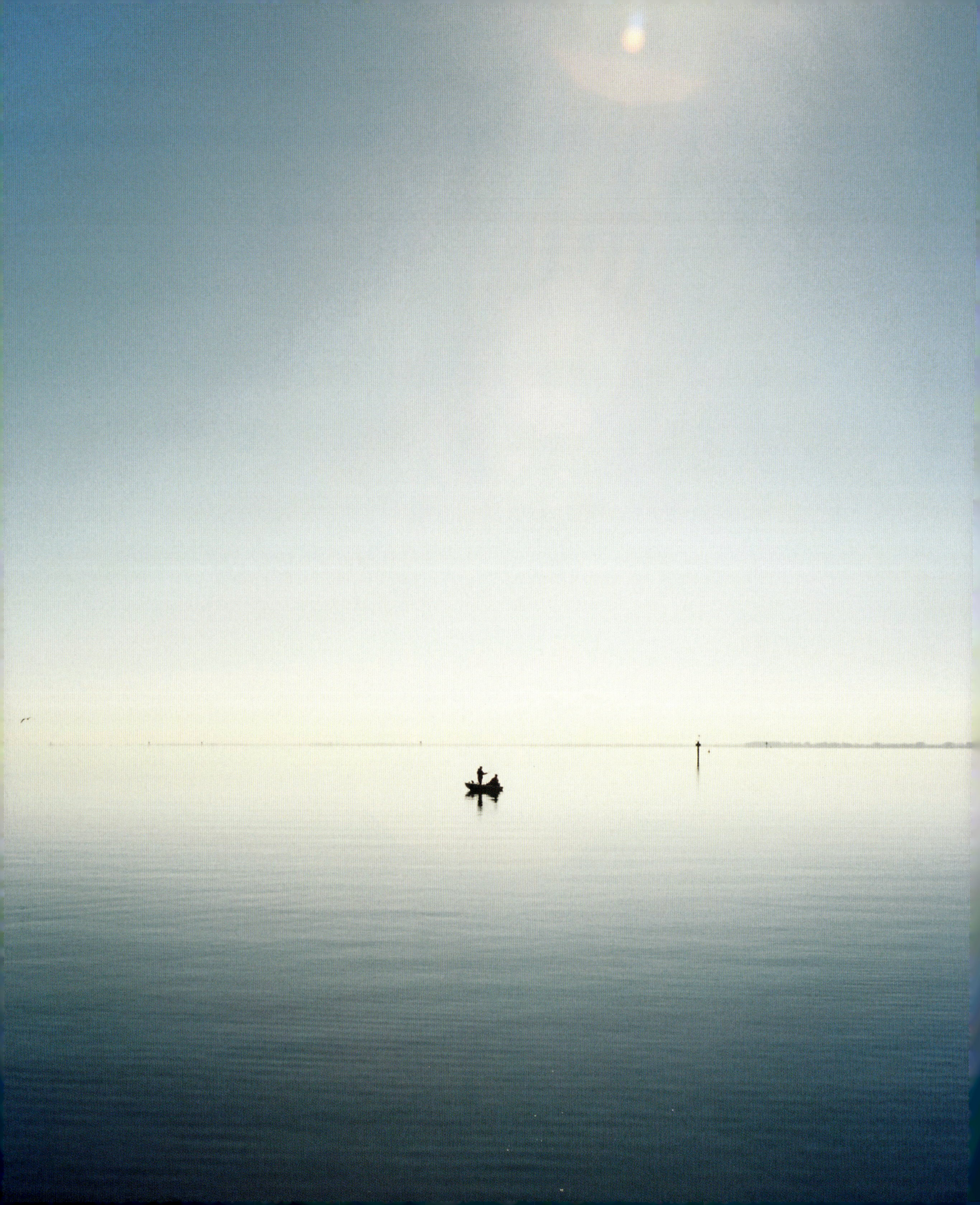

BREATHE

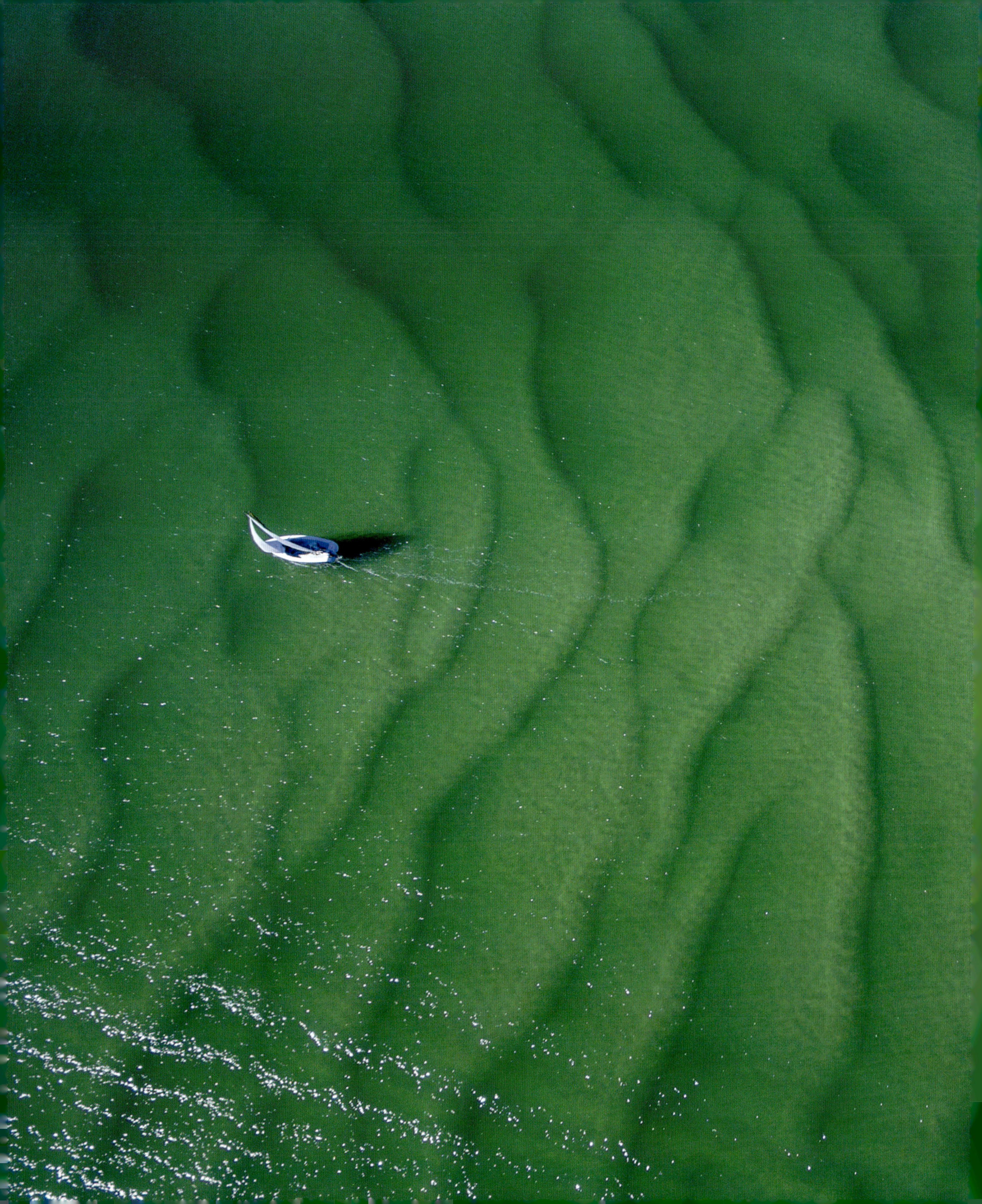

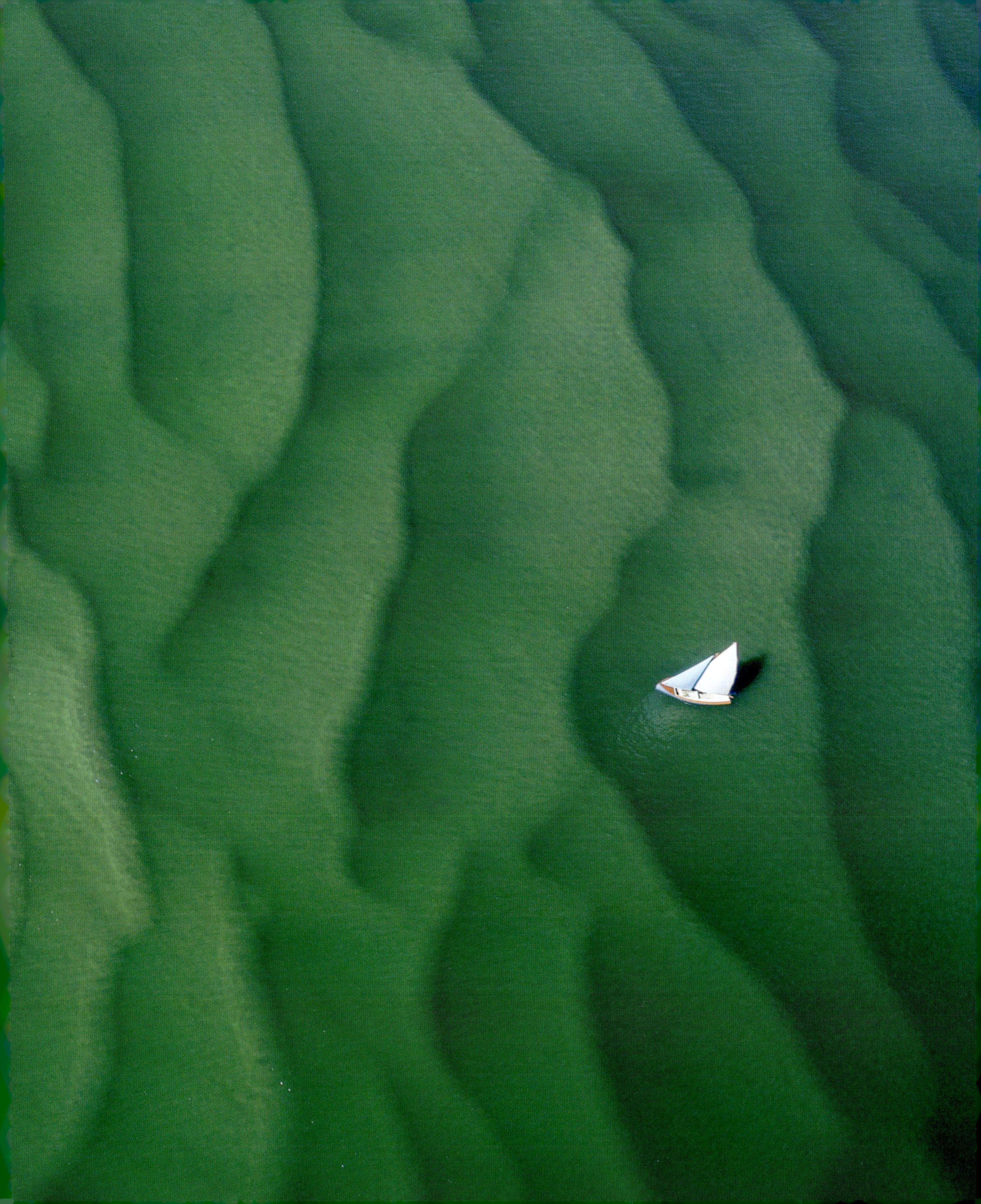

Life at the Edge

Opening Page: Geelong, Victoria
Previous spread: Caloundra, Queensland
Above, left to right: Sydney, New South Wales; Aireys Inlet, Victoria;
Lorne, Victoria; Moreton Island, Queensland

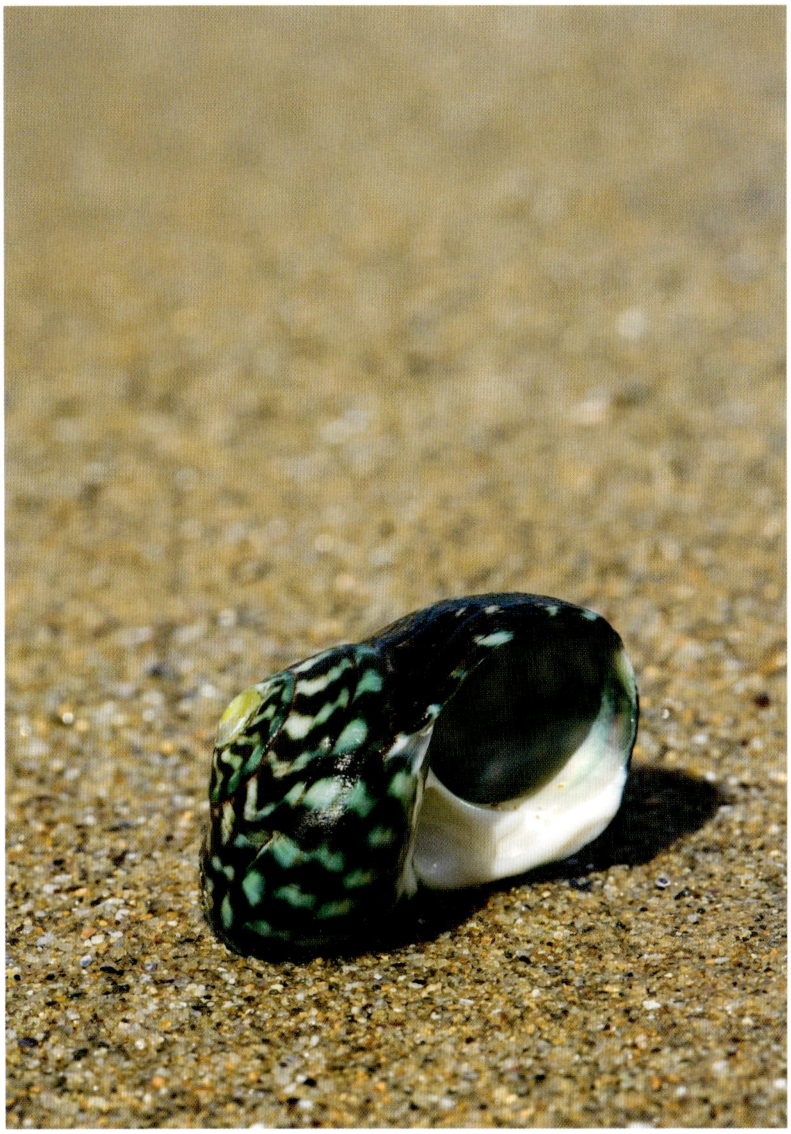

Above: Darwin, Northern Territory
Right: Maroochydore, Queensland

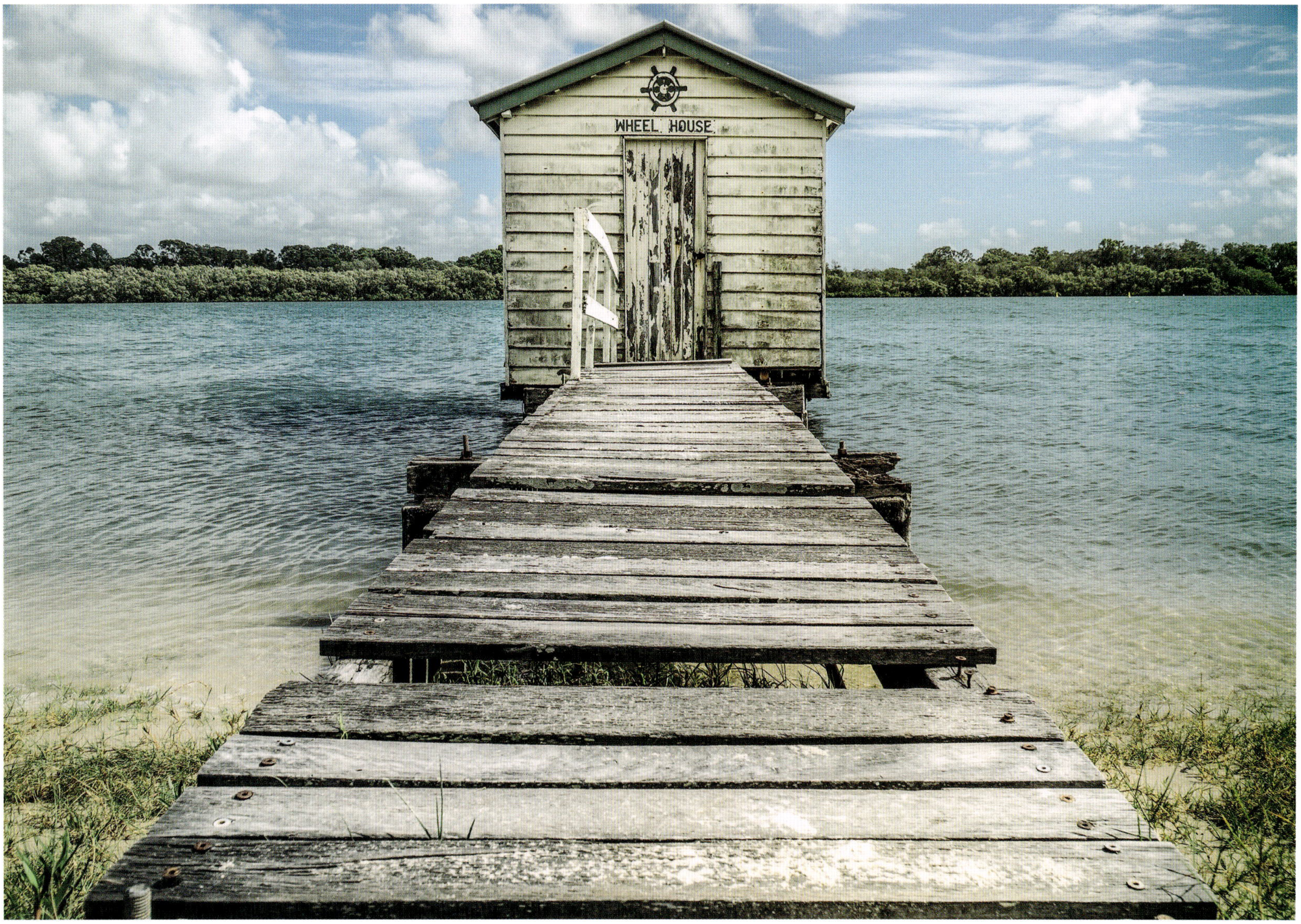
WHEEL HOUSE

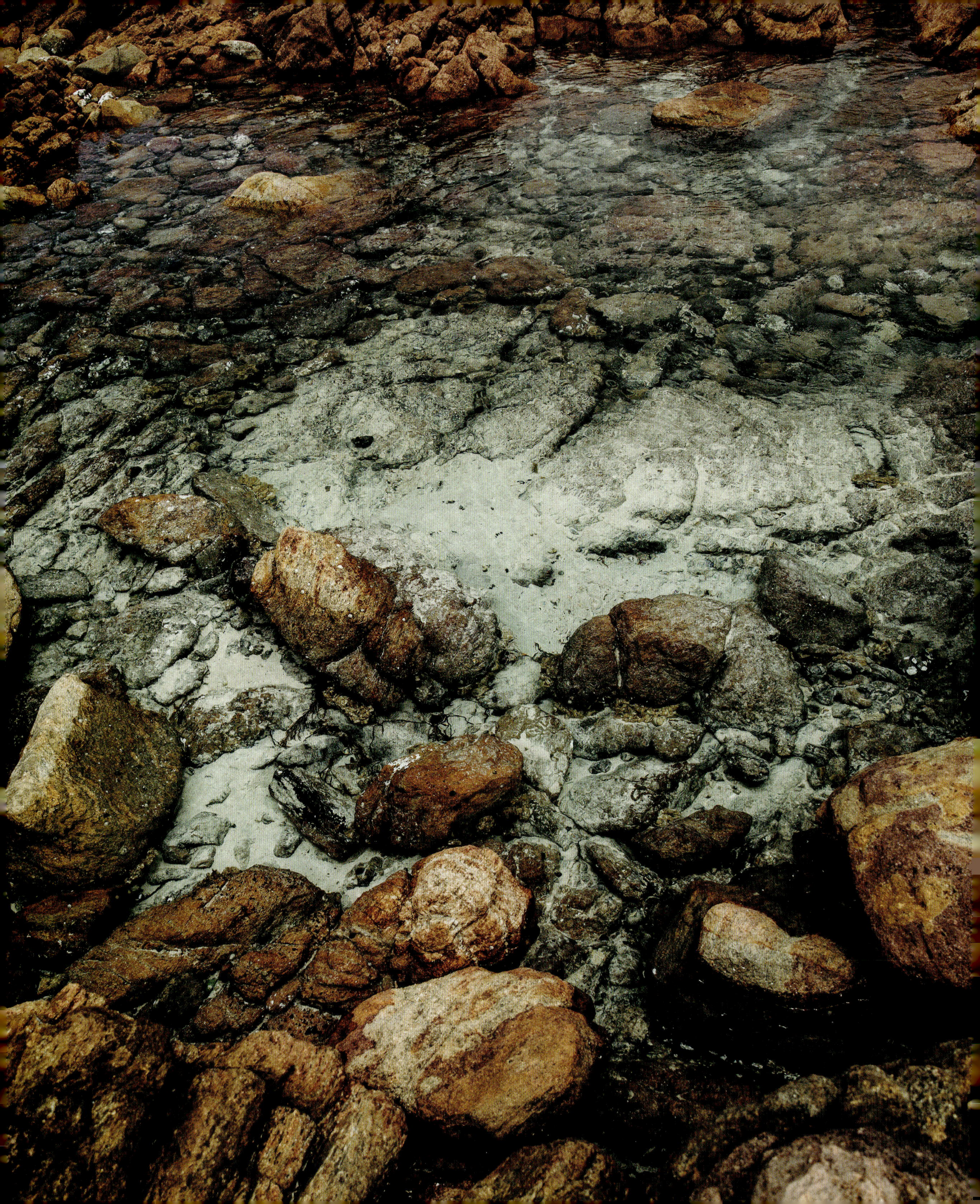

Left: Yallingup, Western Australia
Above: Coalcliff, New South Wales

Life at the Edge

Above: Mount Wellington, Tasmania
Right: Buccaneer Archipelago, Western Australia

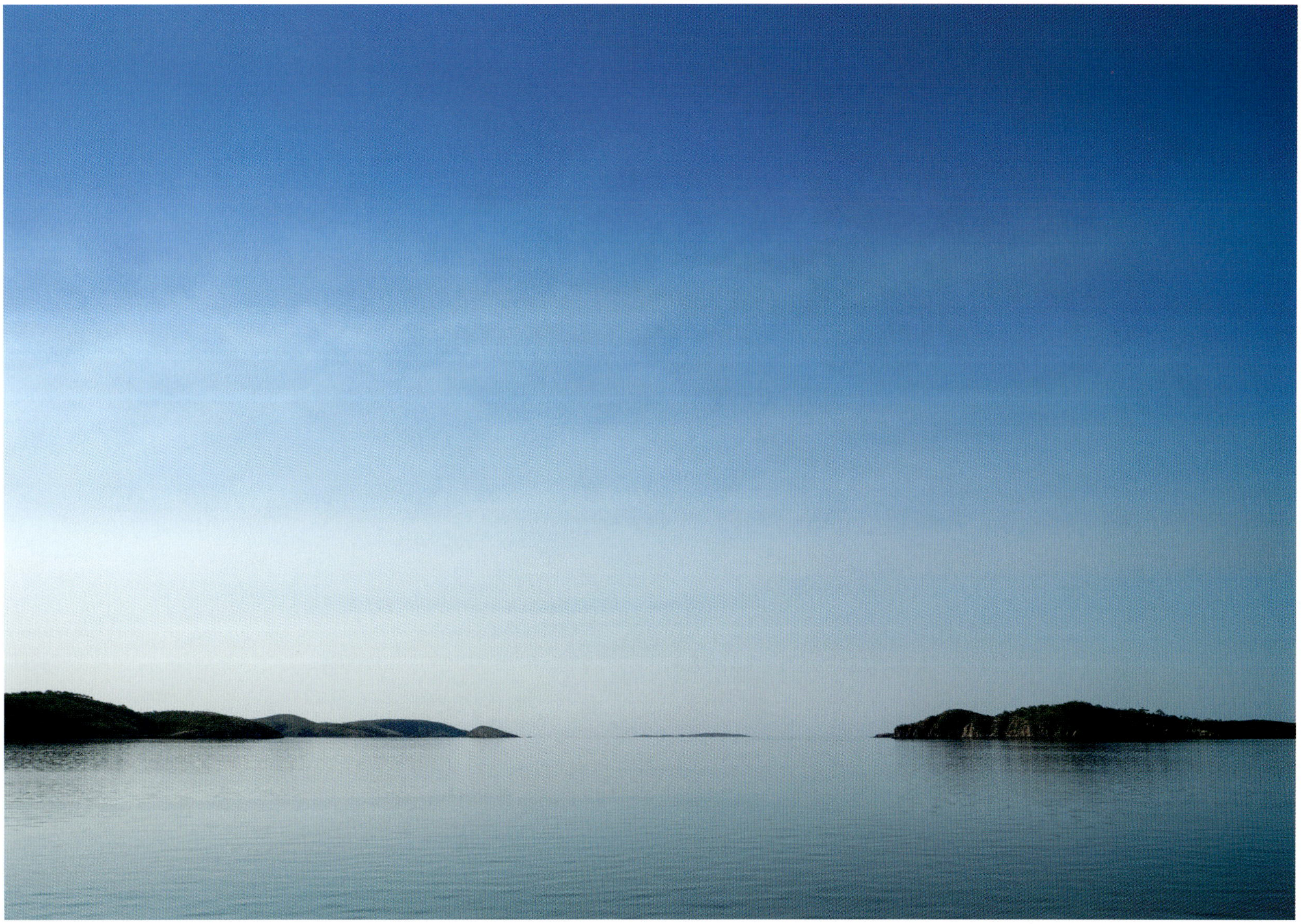

Life at the Edge

Kakadu National Park, Northern Territory

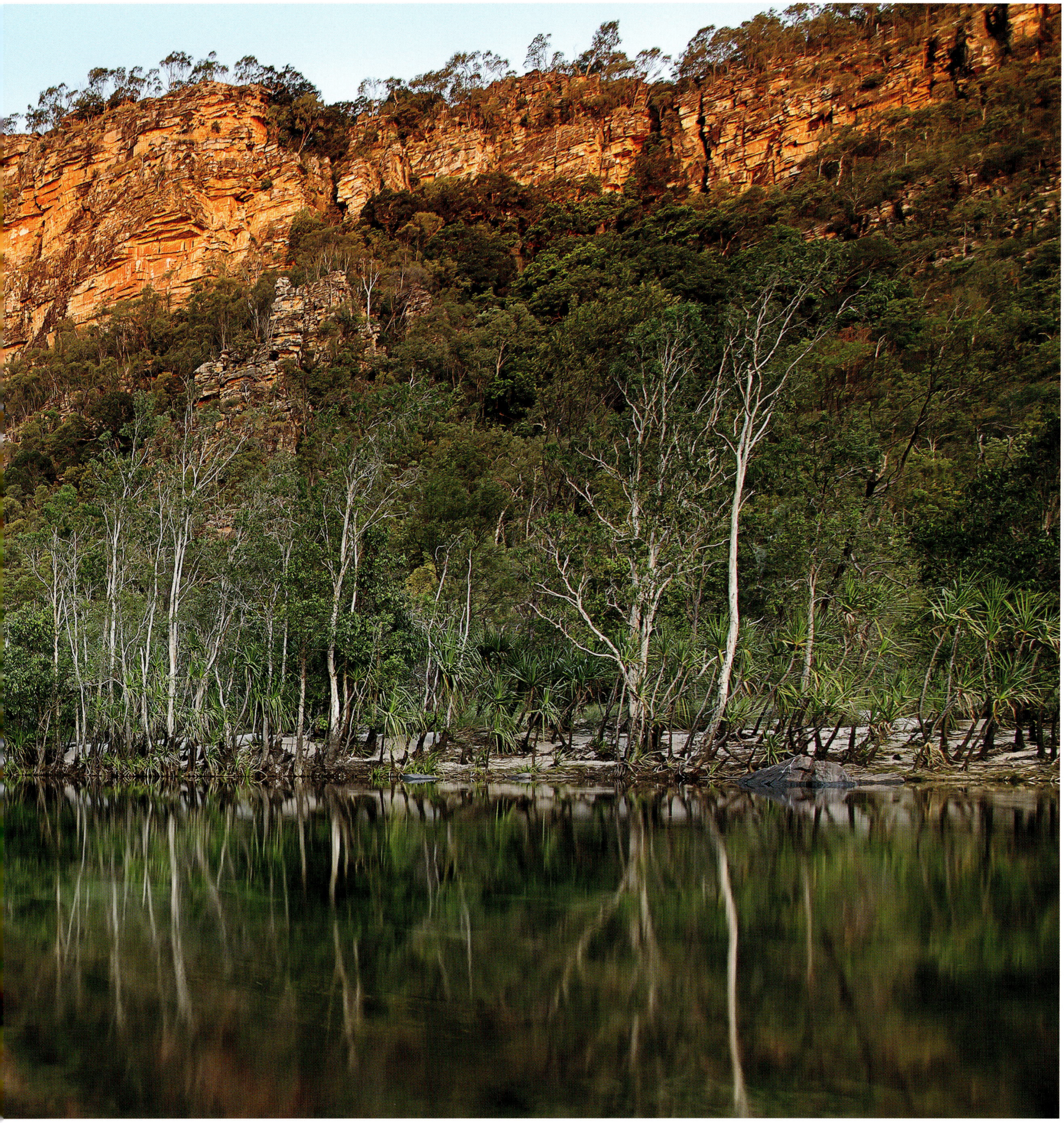

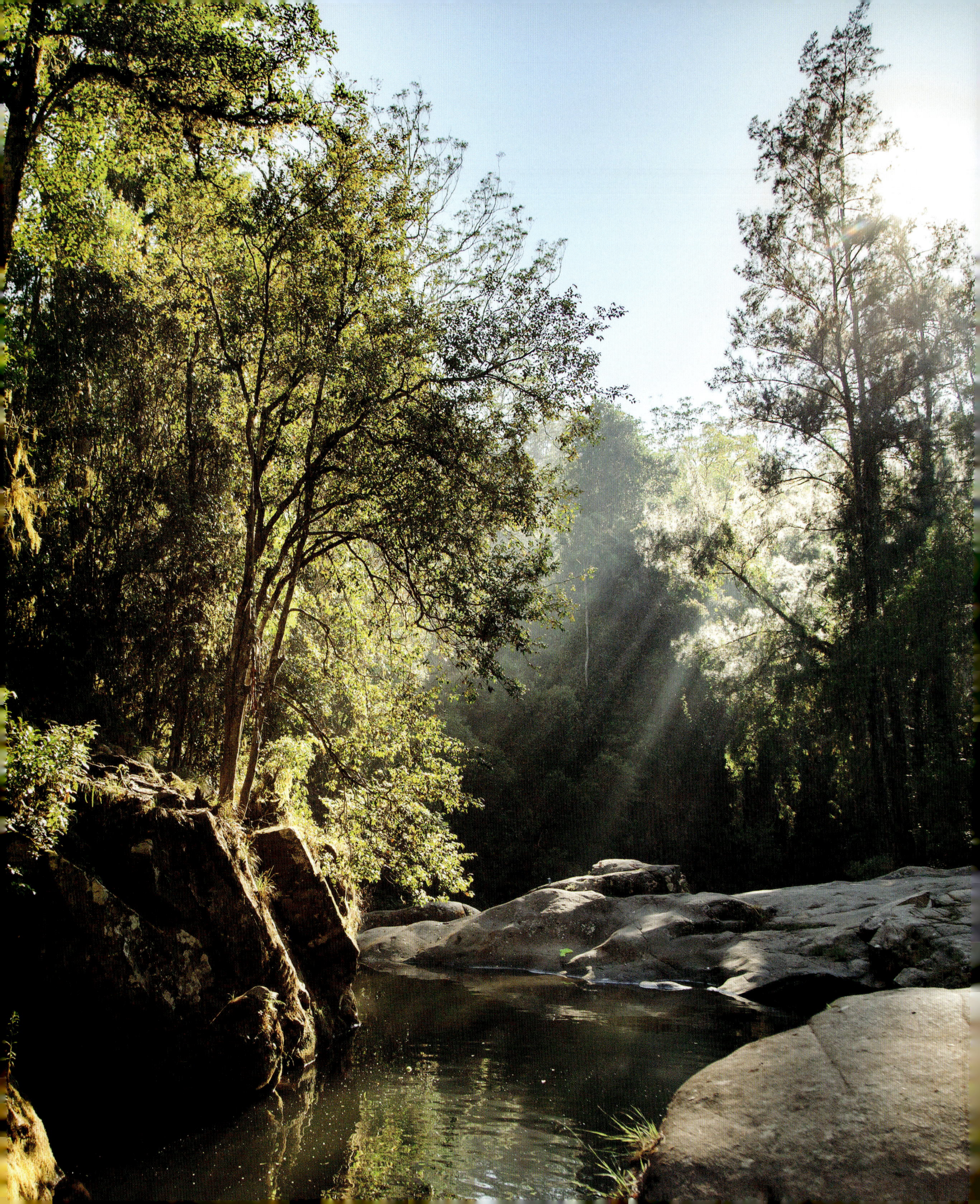

Left: Dungog, New South Wales
Above: Pemberton, Western Australia

Above, left to right: North Beach, Western Australia; Barwon Heads, Victoria
Following spread: Babinda, Queensland

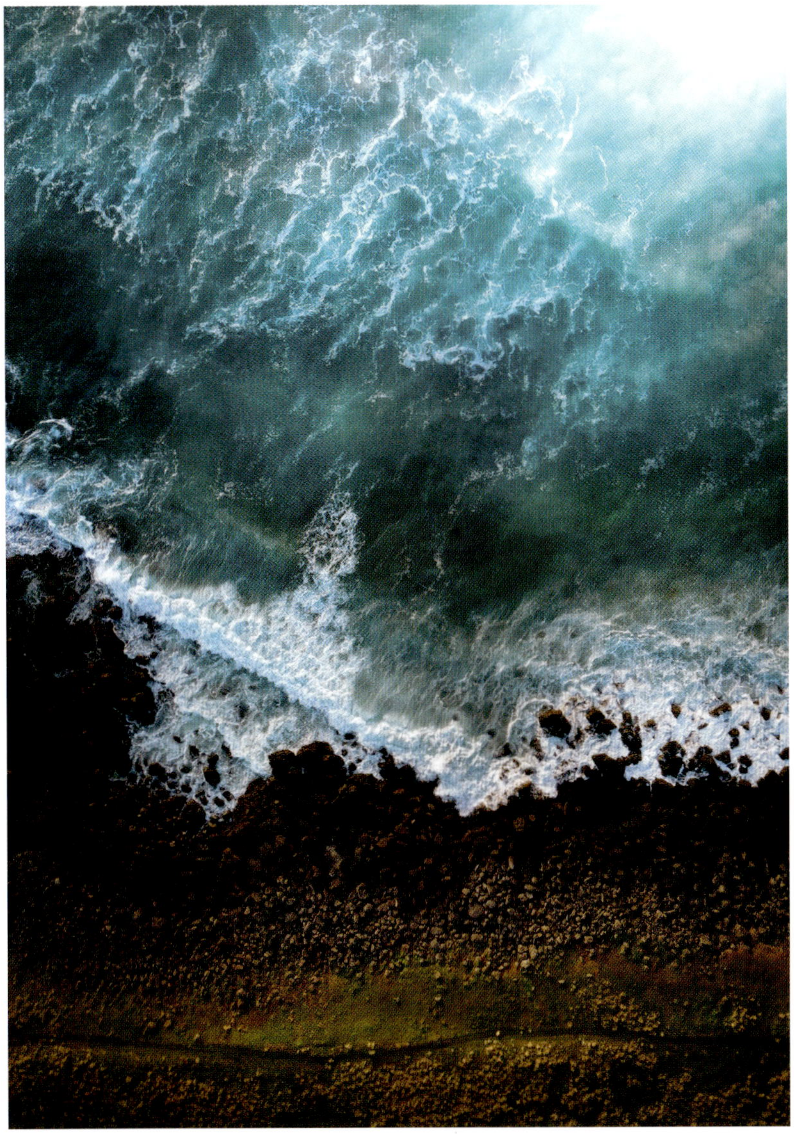

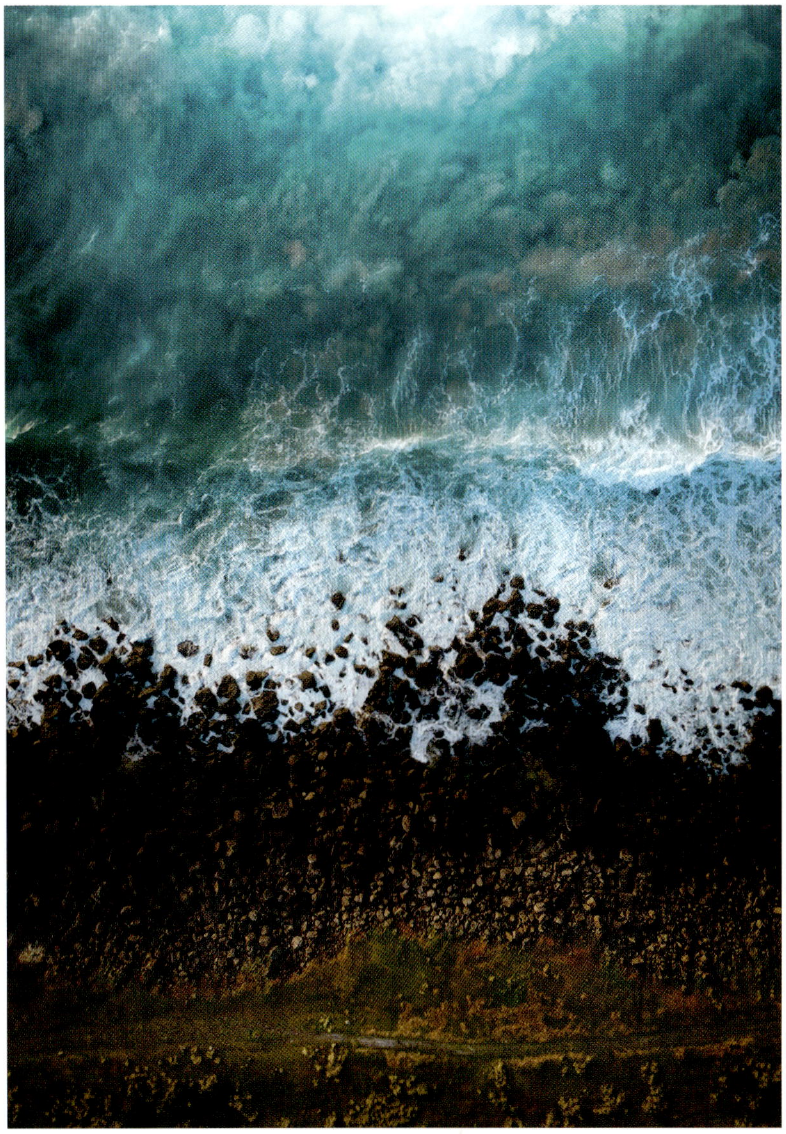

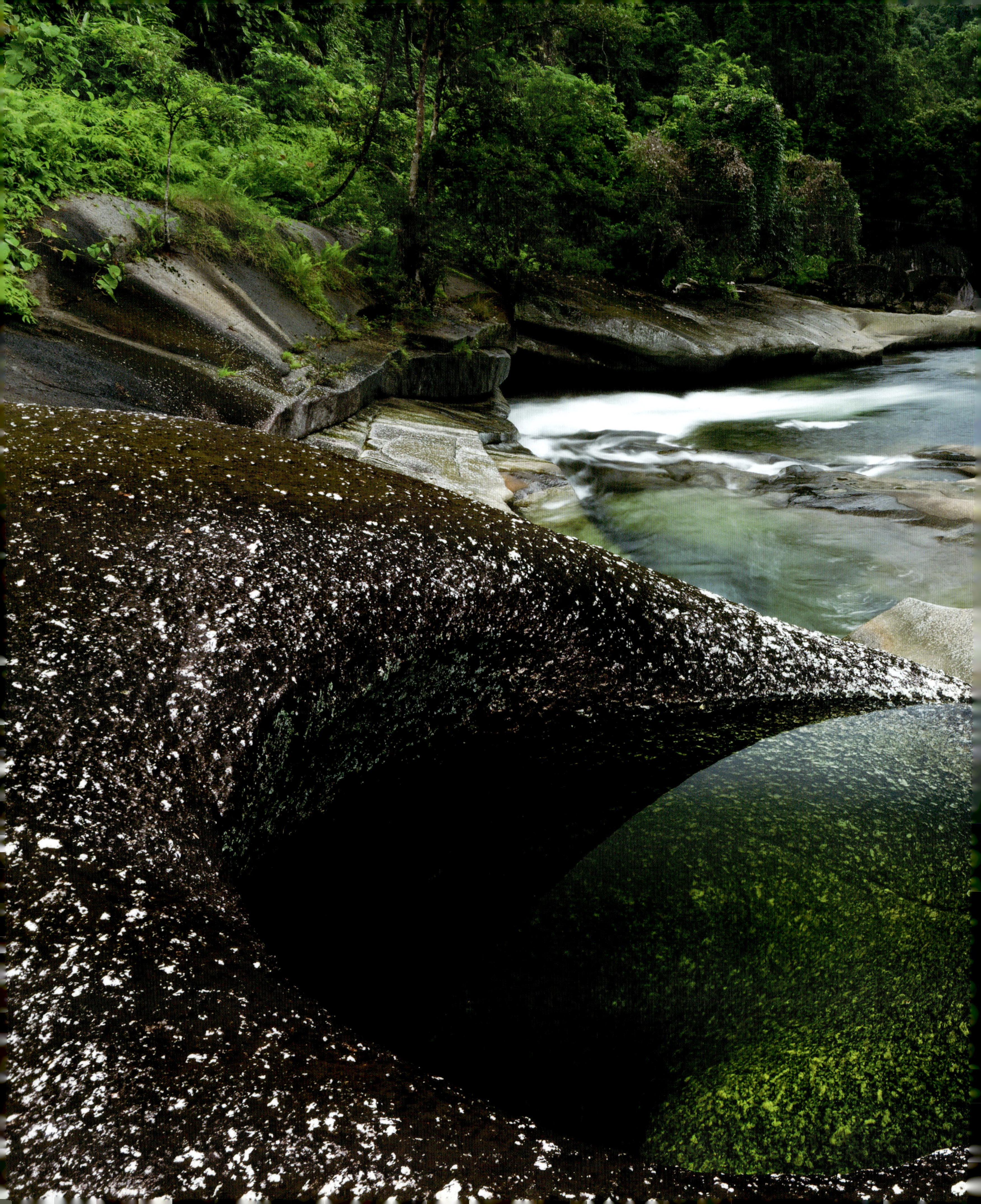

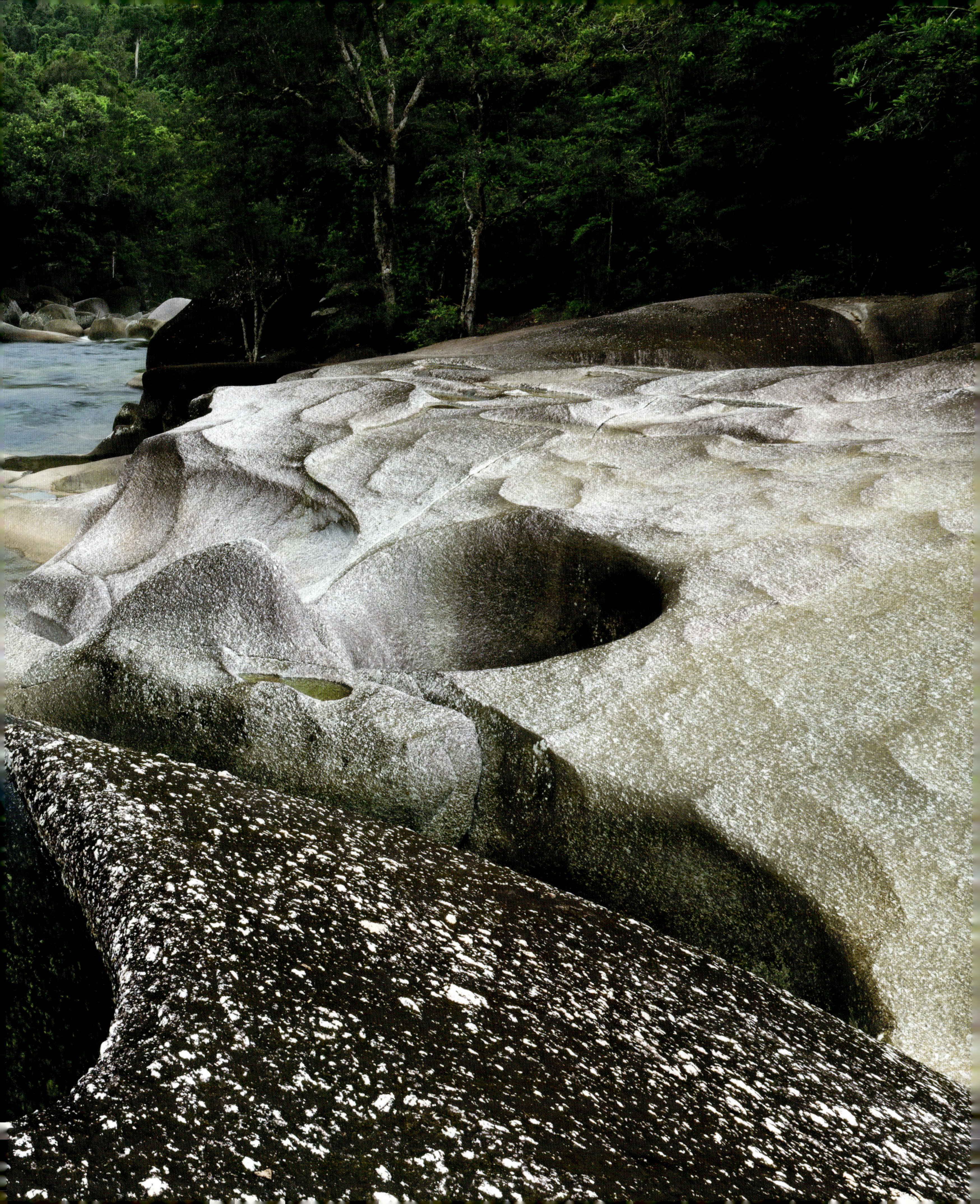

Above: Dungog, New South Wales
Right: Wildes Meadow, New South Wales

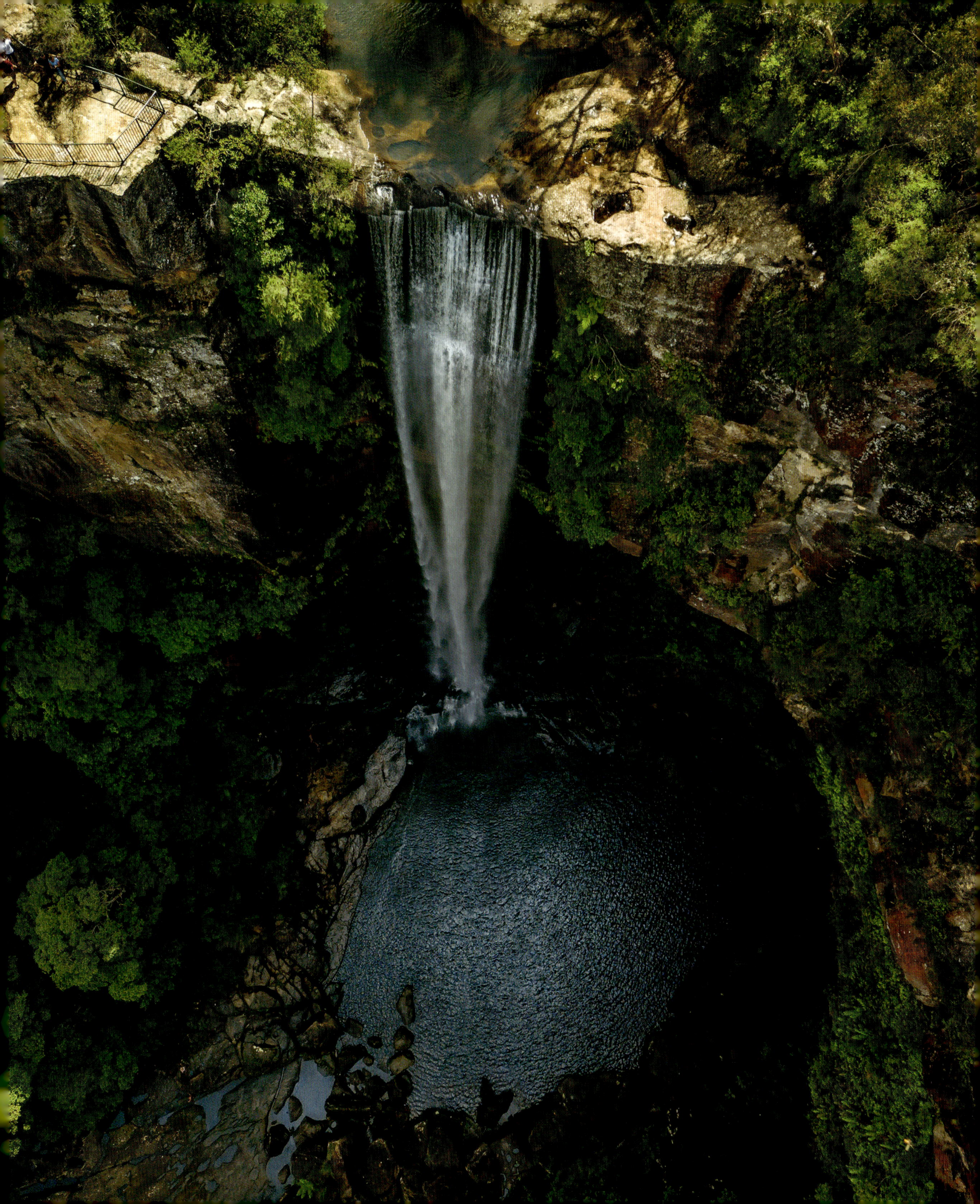

Life at the Edge

Gulf St Vincent, South Australia

Breathe

Life at the Edge

Above: Buffalo Creek, Northern Territory
Right: Gloucester, New South Wales

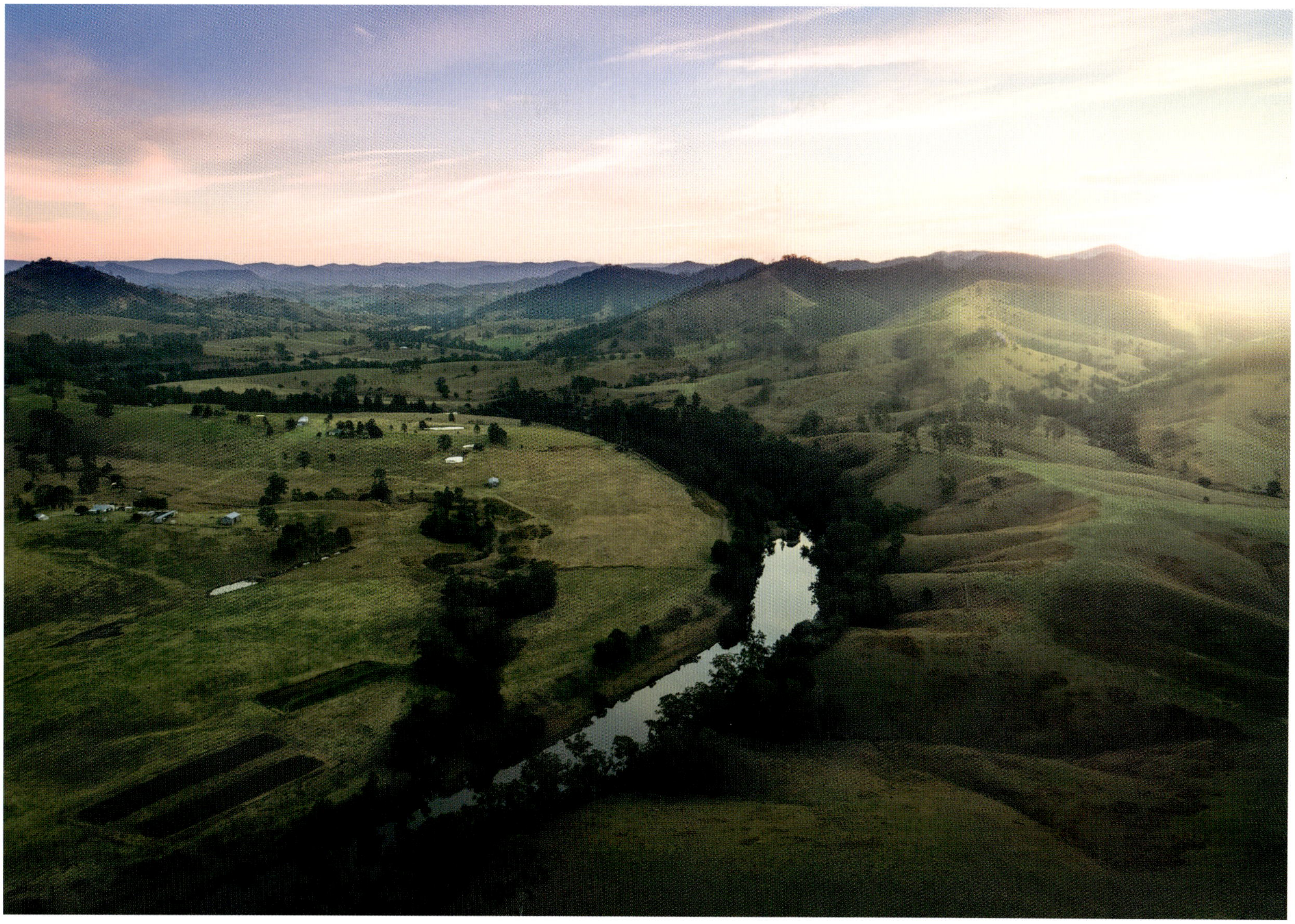

Life at the Edge

Above: Denmark, Western Australia
Right: Pemberton, Western Australia

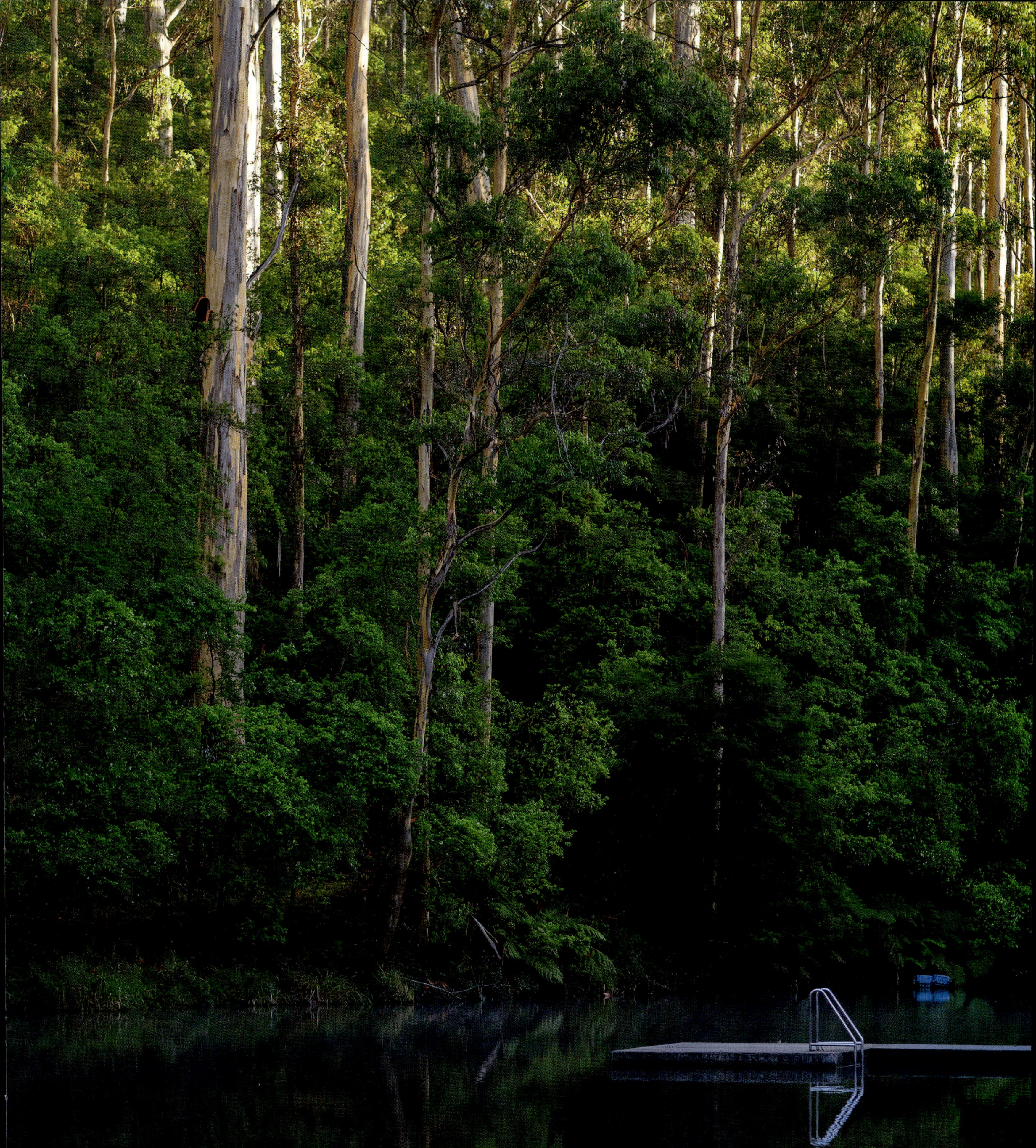

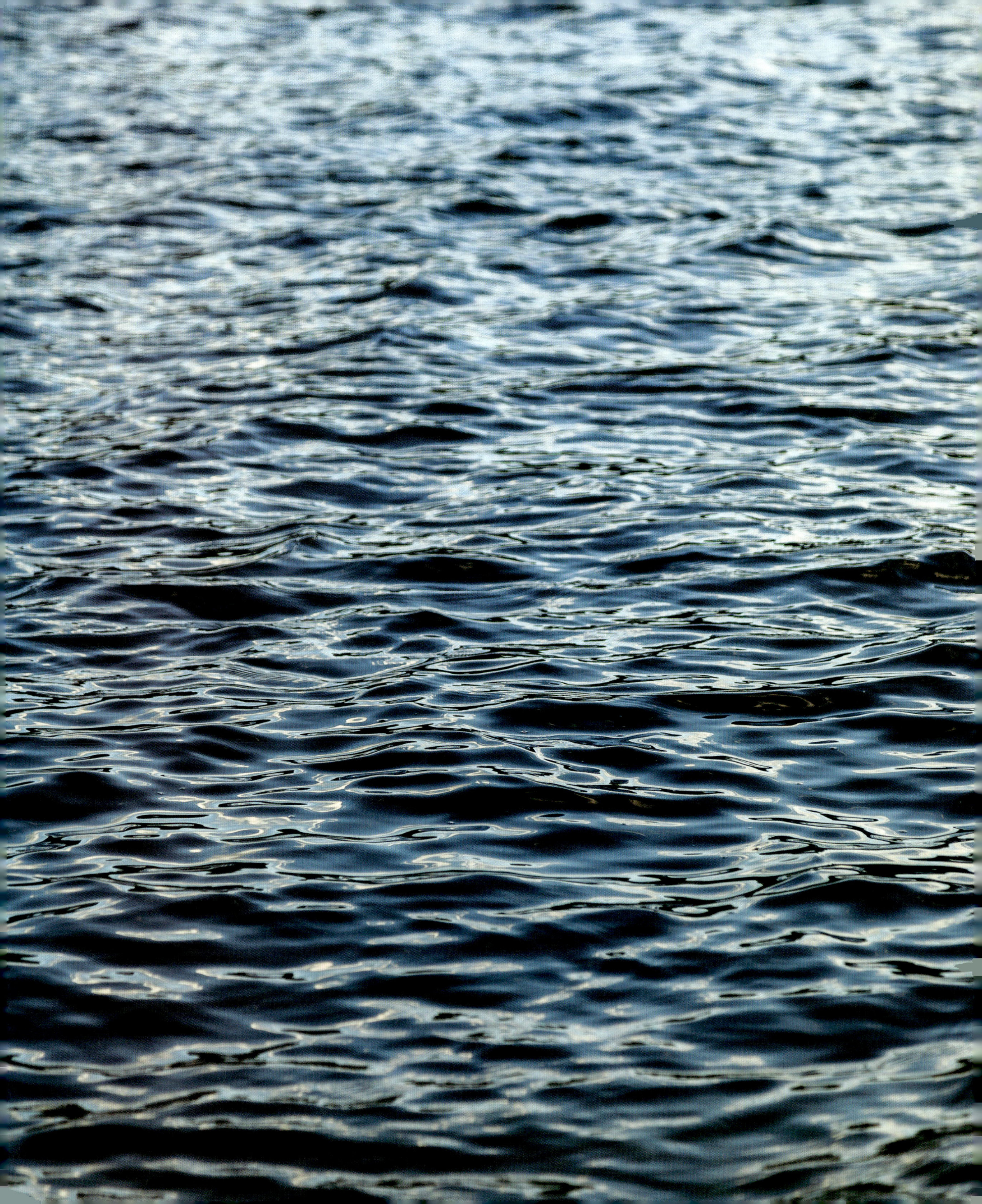

Left: Talbingo, New South Wales
Above: Double Bay, New South Wales
Following spread: Kakadu National Park, Northern Territory

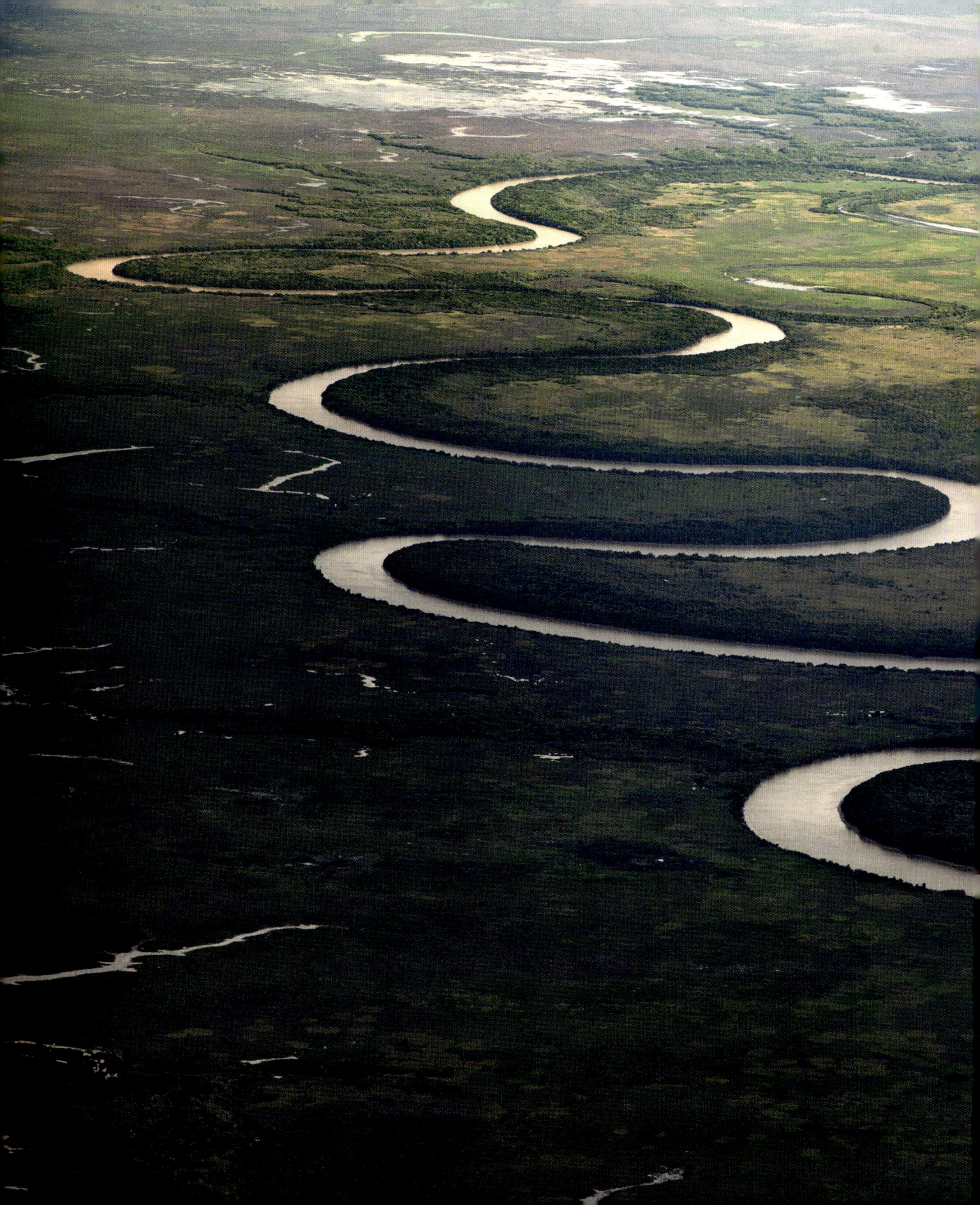

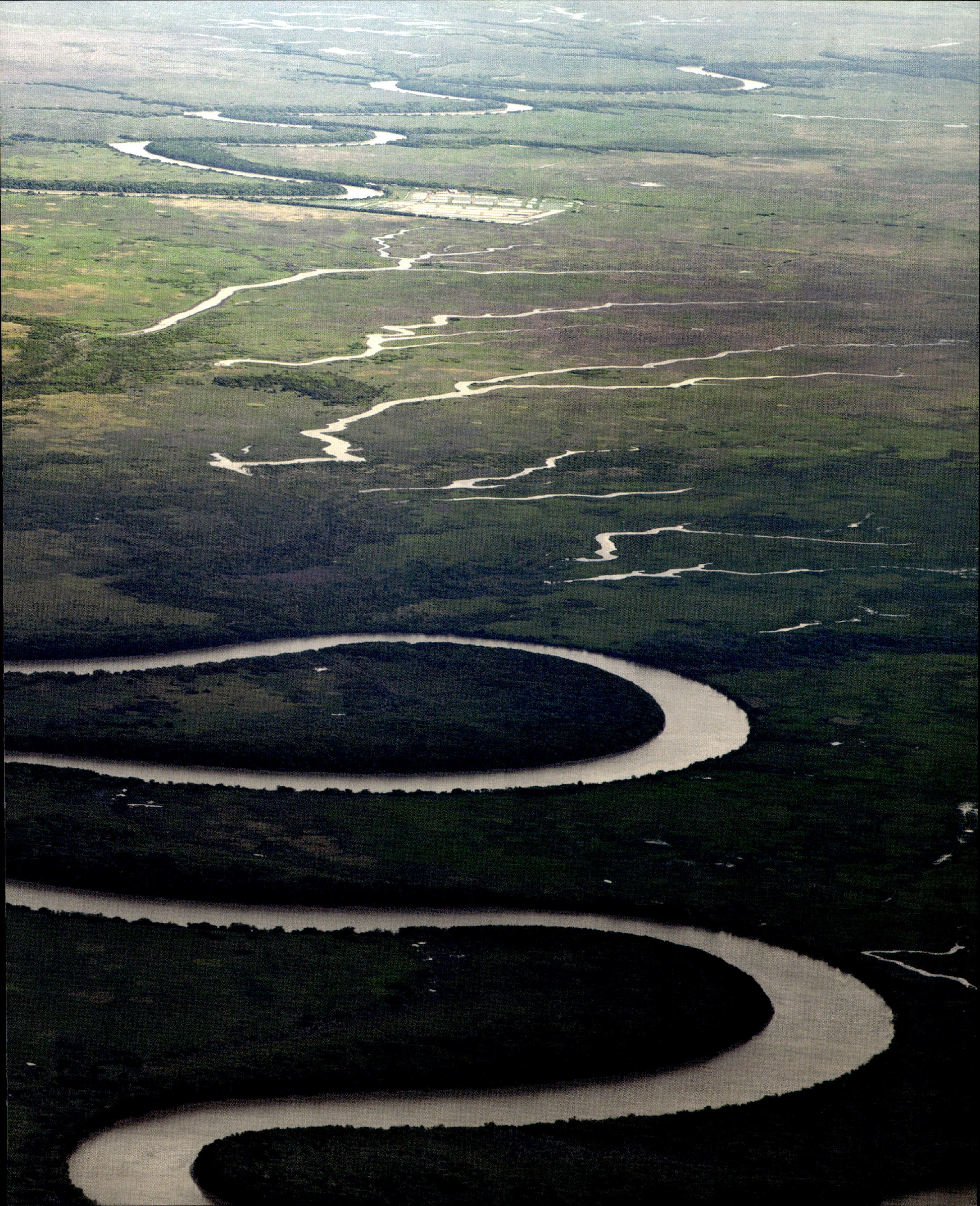

Adelaide Hills, South Australia

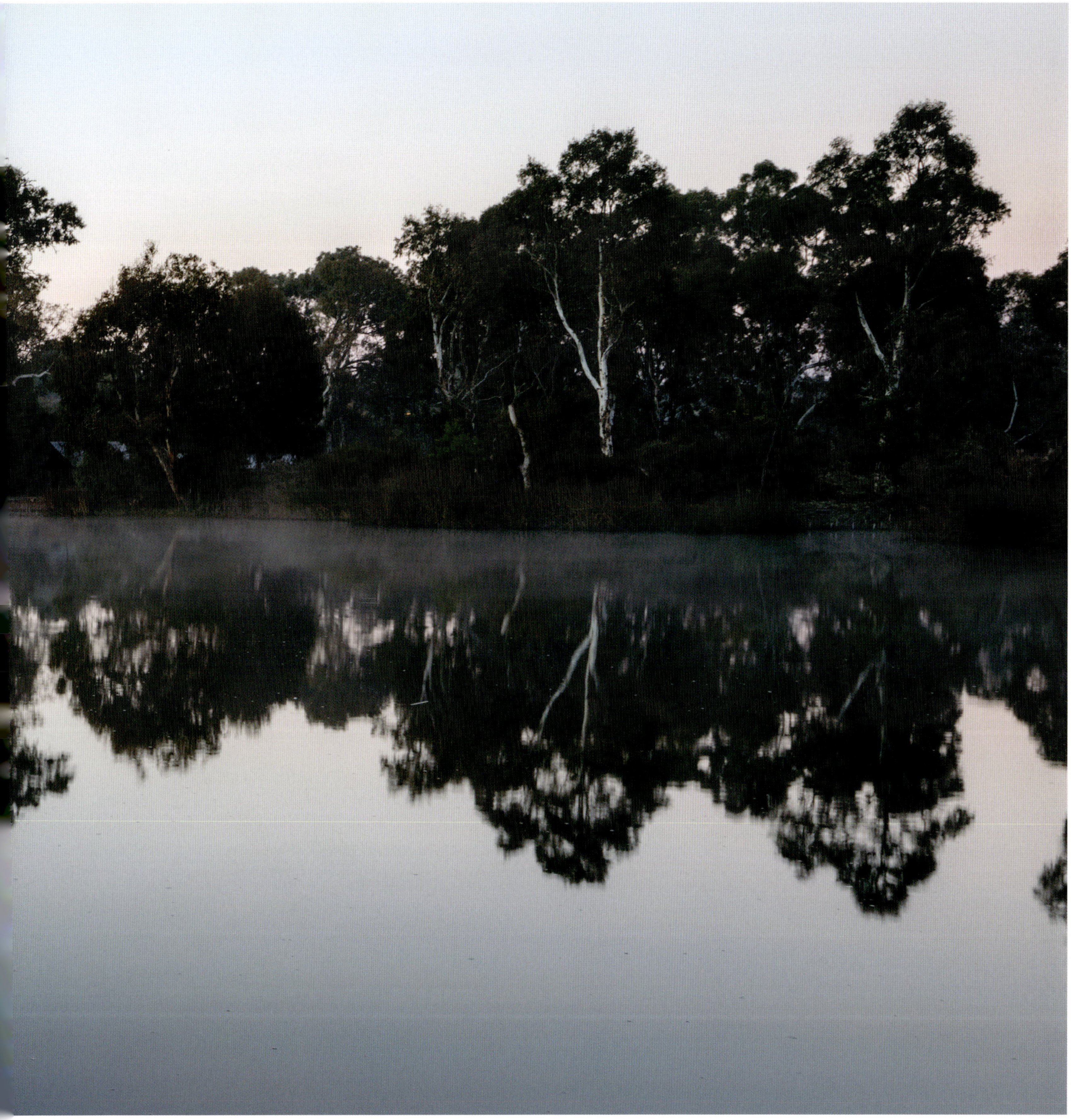

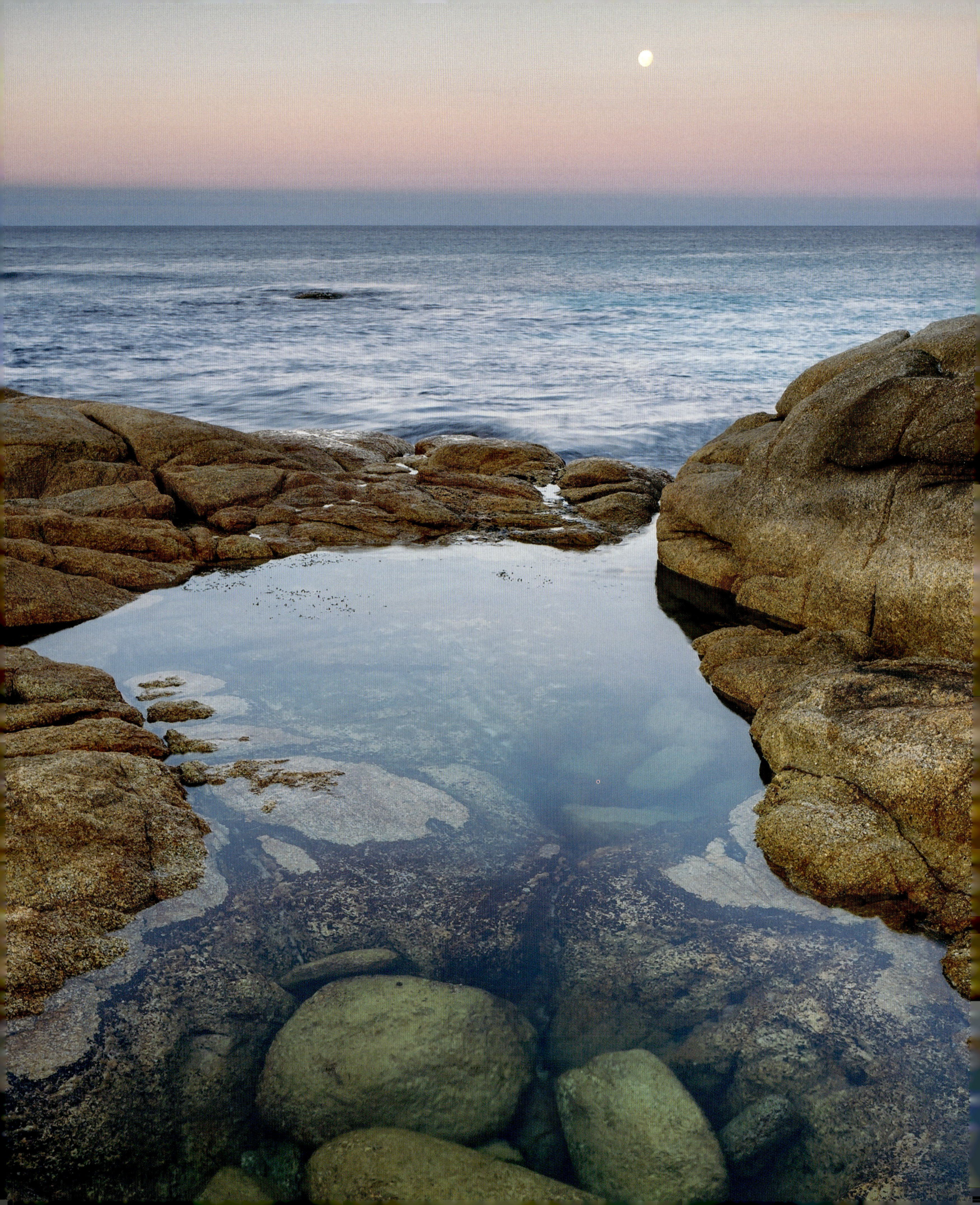

Left: Binalong Bay, Tasmania
Above, left to right: Binalong Bay, Tasmania.; Aireys Inlet, Victoria

Life at the Edge

Above: Bremer Bay, Western Australia
Right: Melbourne, Victoria

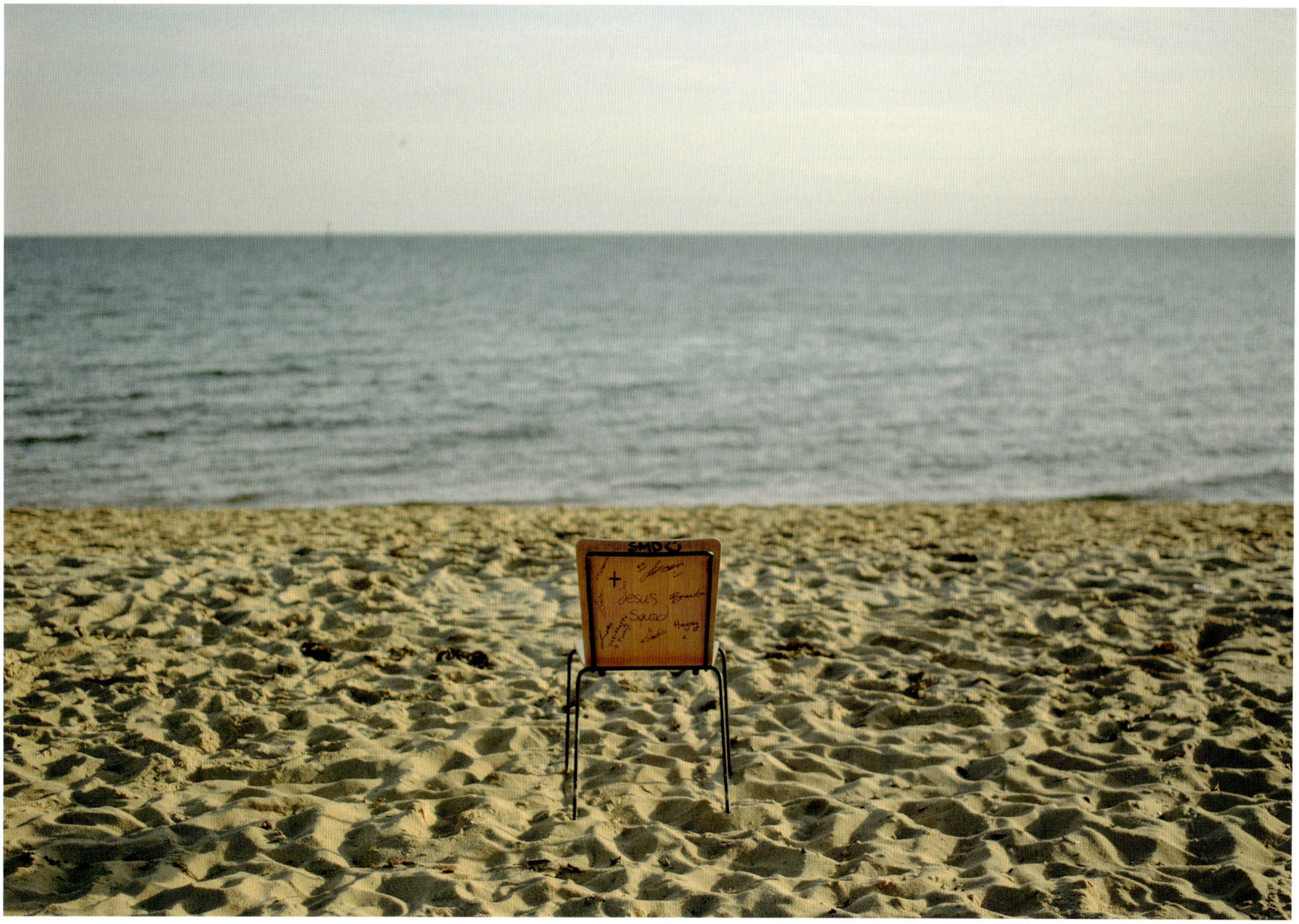
Jesus
Squad

Life at the Edge

Above: Terrigal, New South Wales
Following spread: Adventure Bay, Tasmania

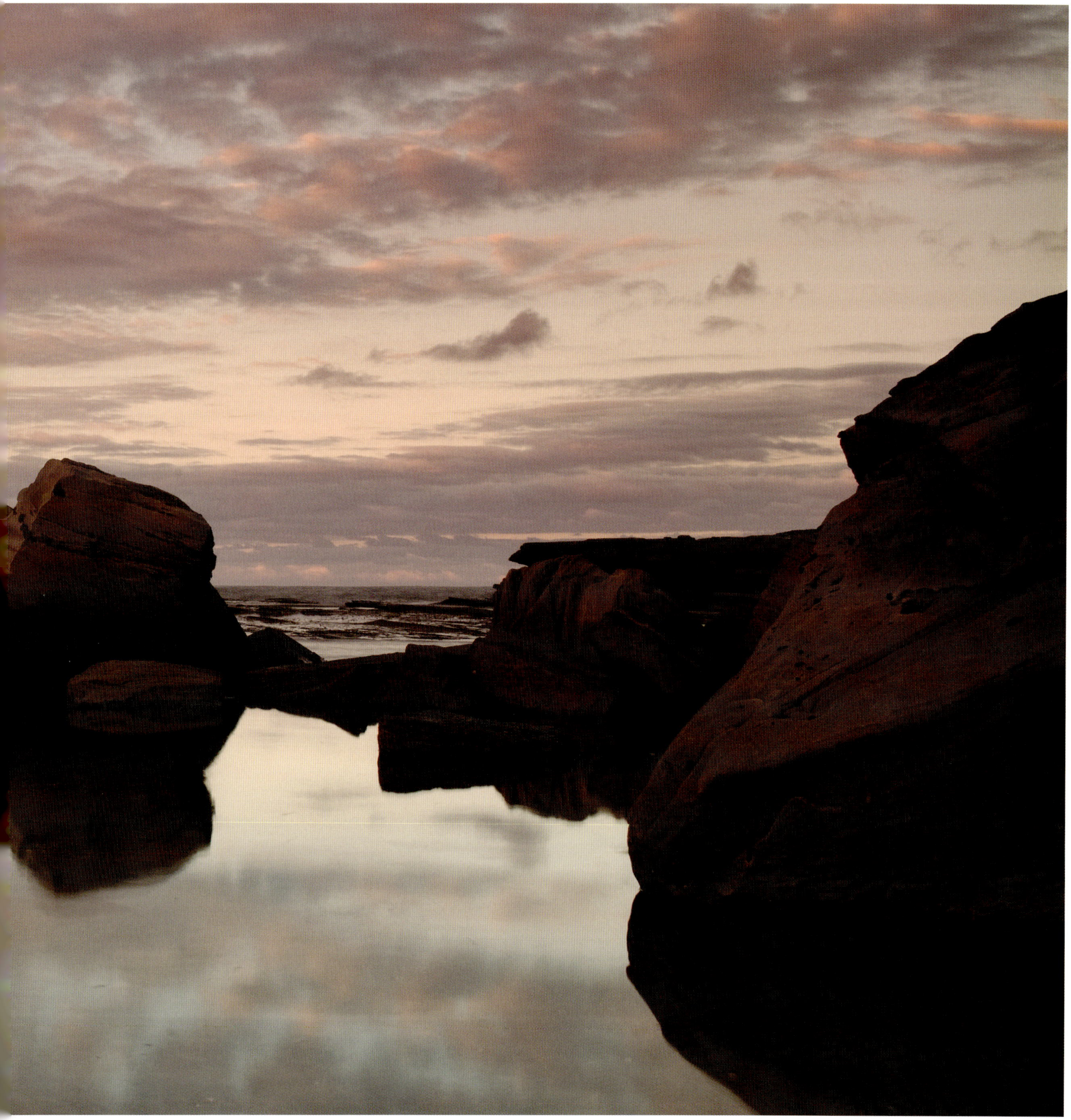

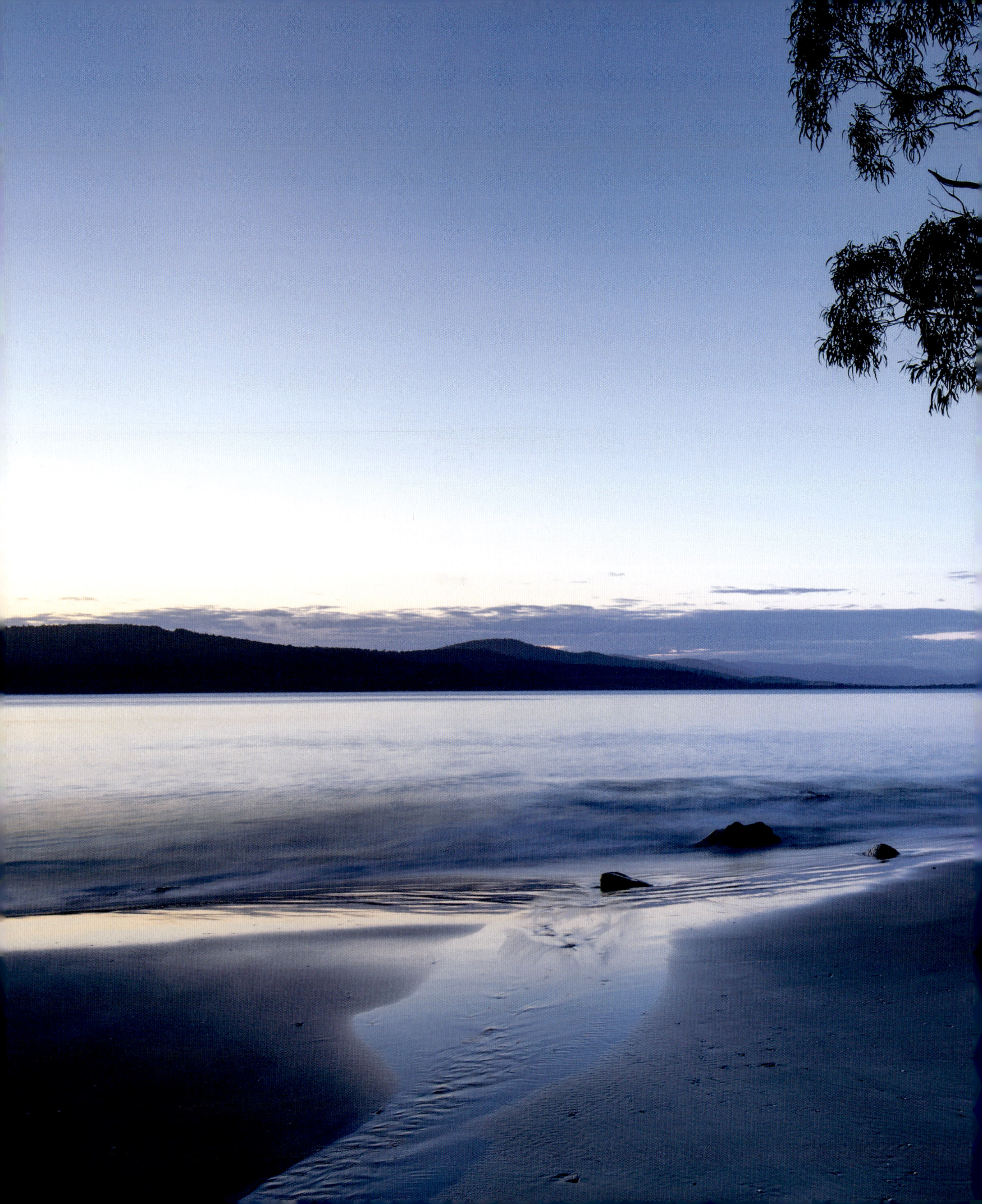

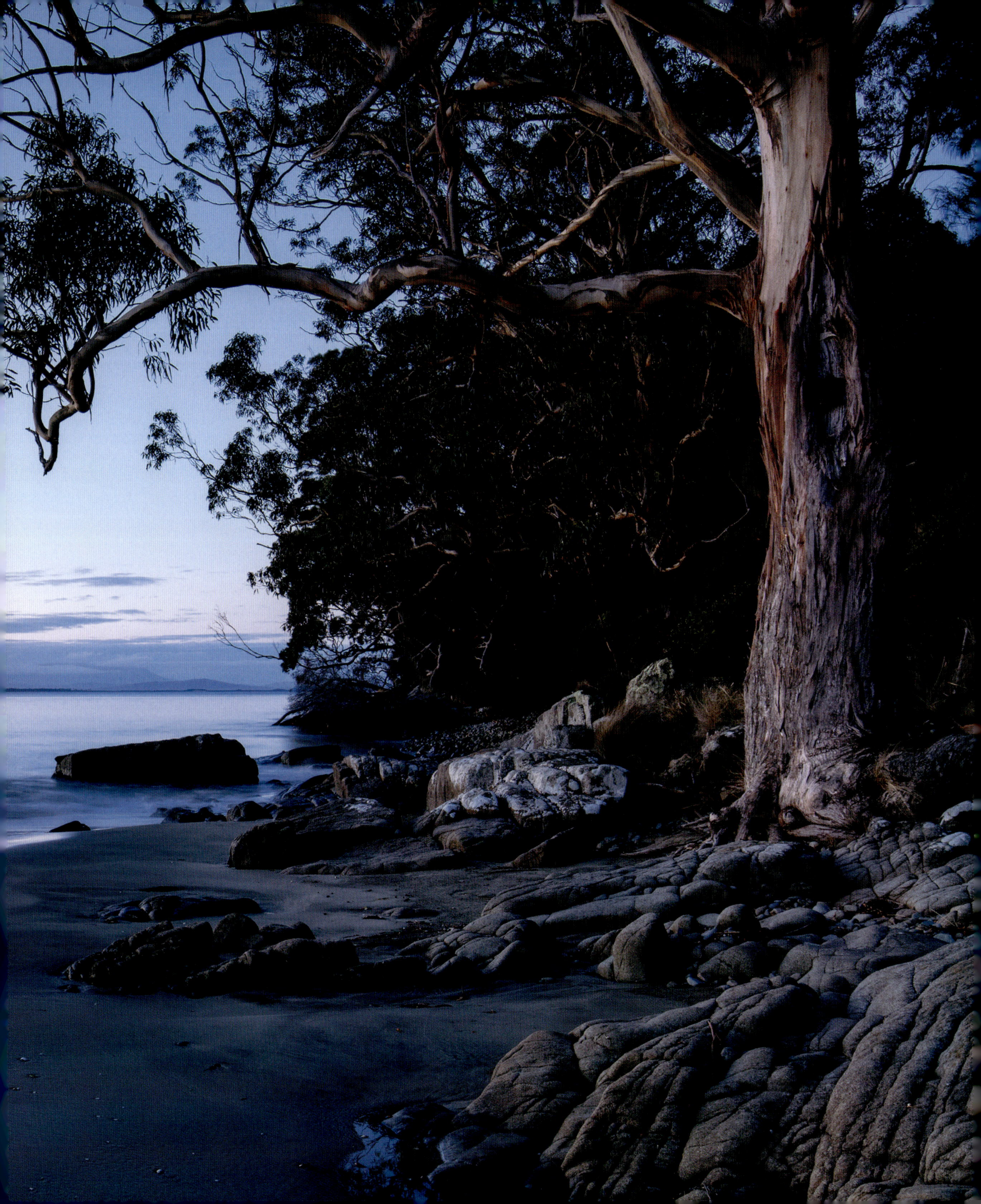

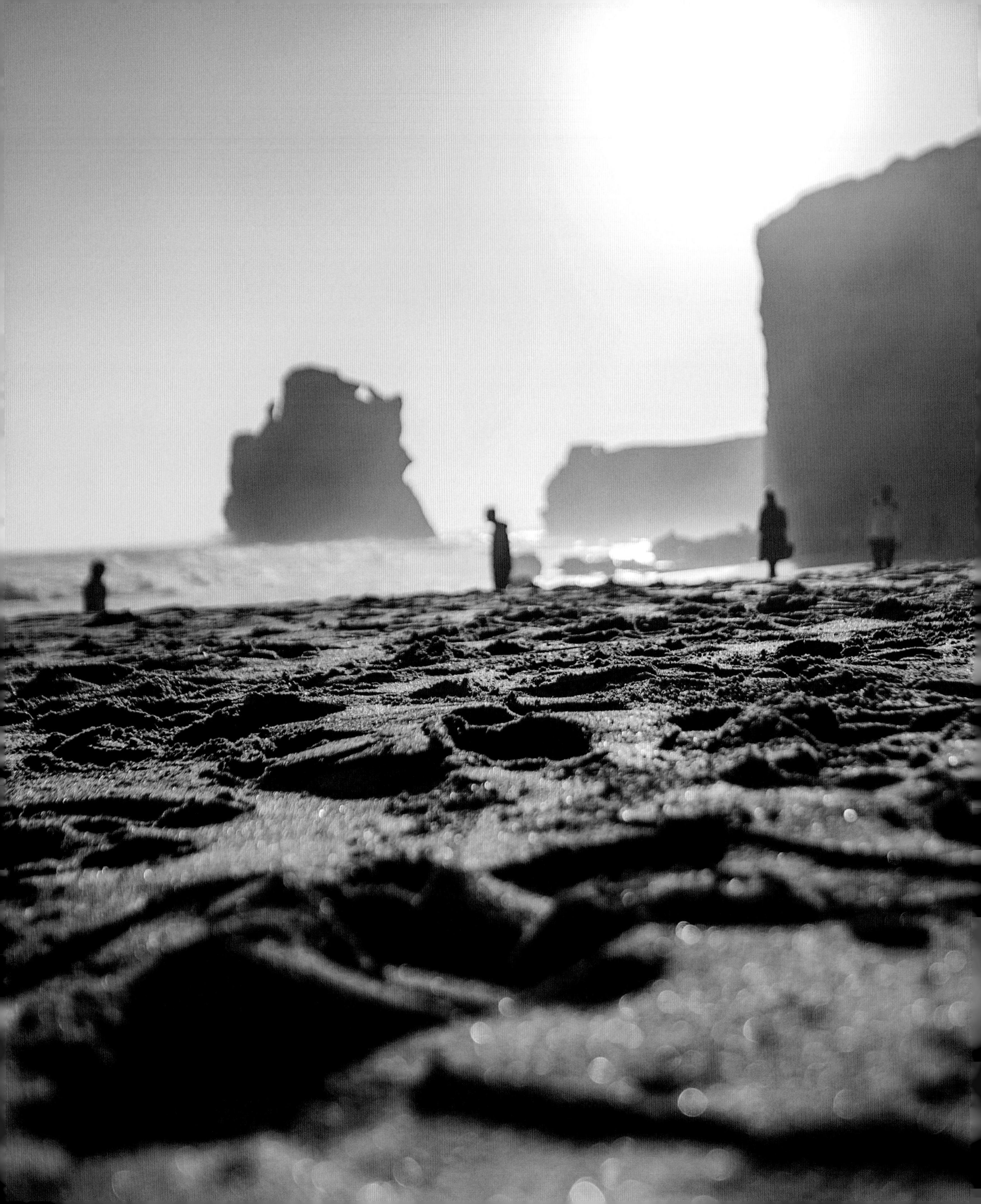

DIS CO VER

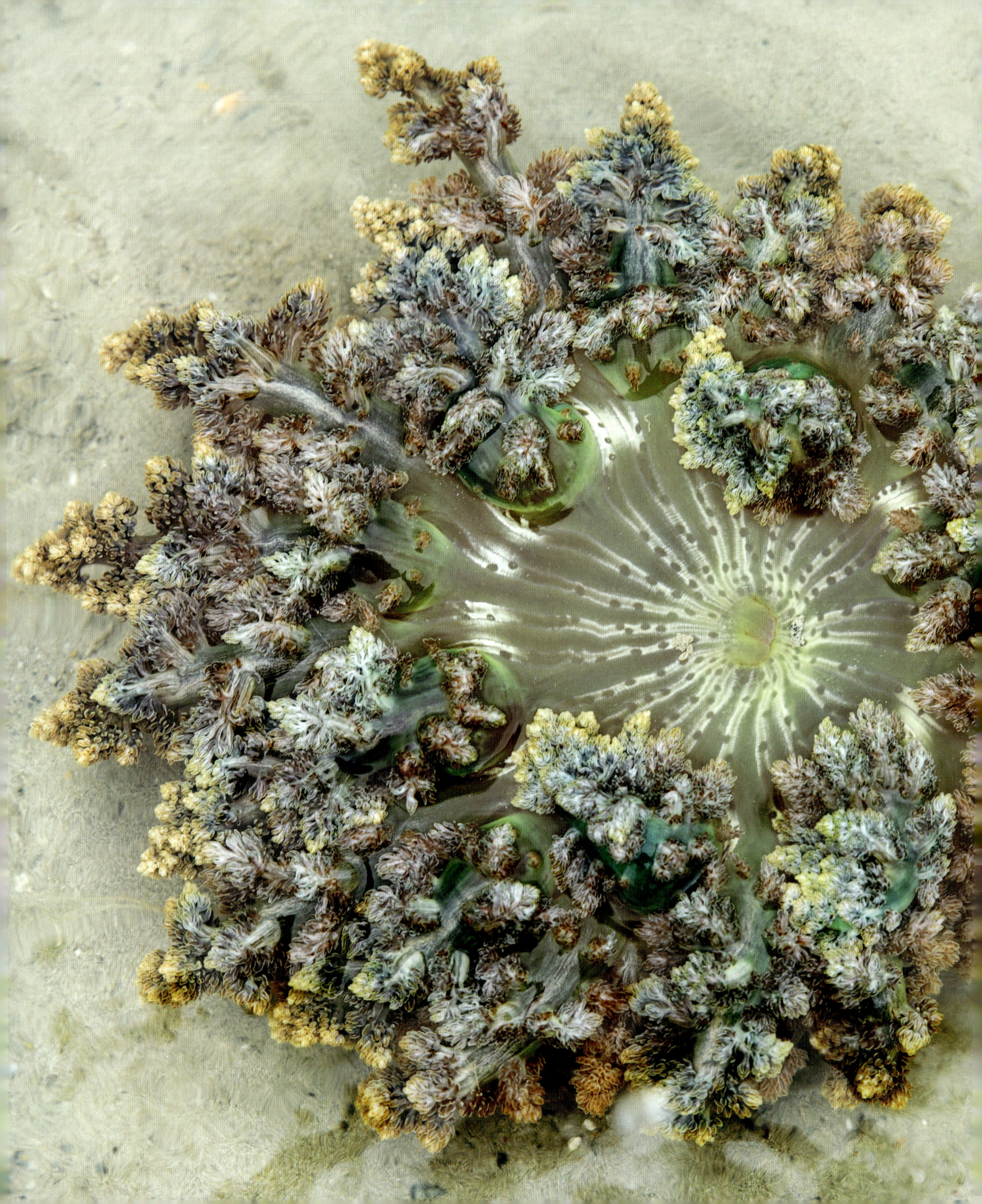

Opening page: Port Campbell, Victoria
Left: Hamilton Island, Queensland
Above: Ningaloo Coast, Western Australia

Above: Sorrento, Western Australia
Right: Melbourne, Victoria

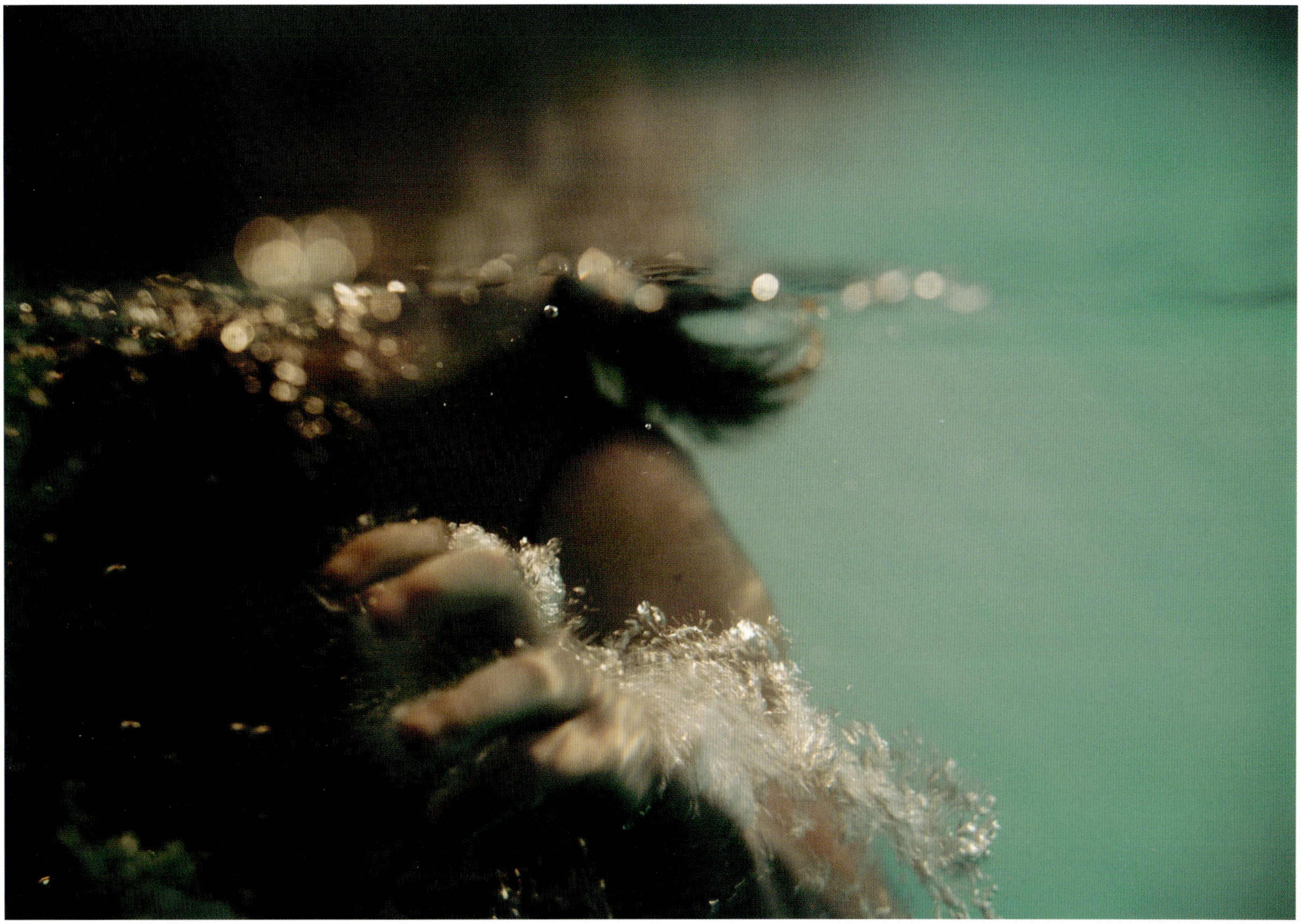

Life at the Edge

Left to right: Hamilton Island, Queensland; Whitsunday Islands, Queensland;
Caves Beach, New South Wales

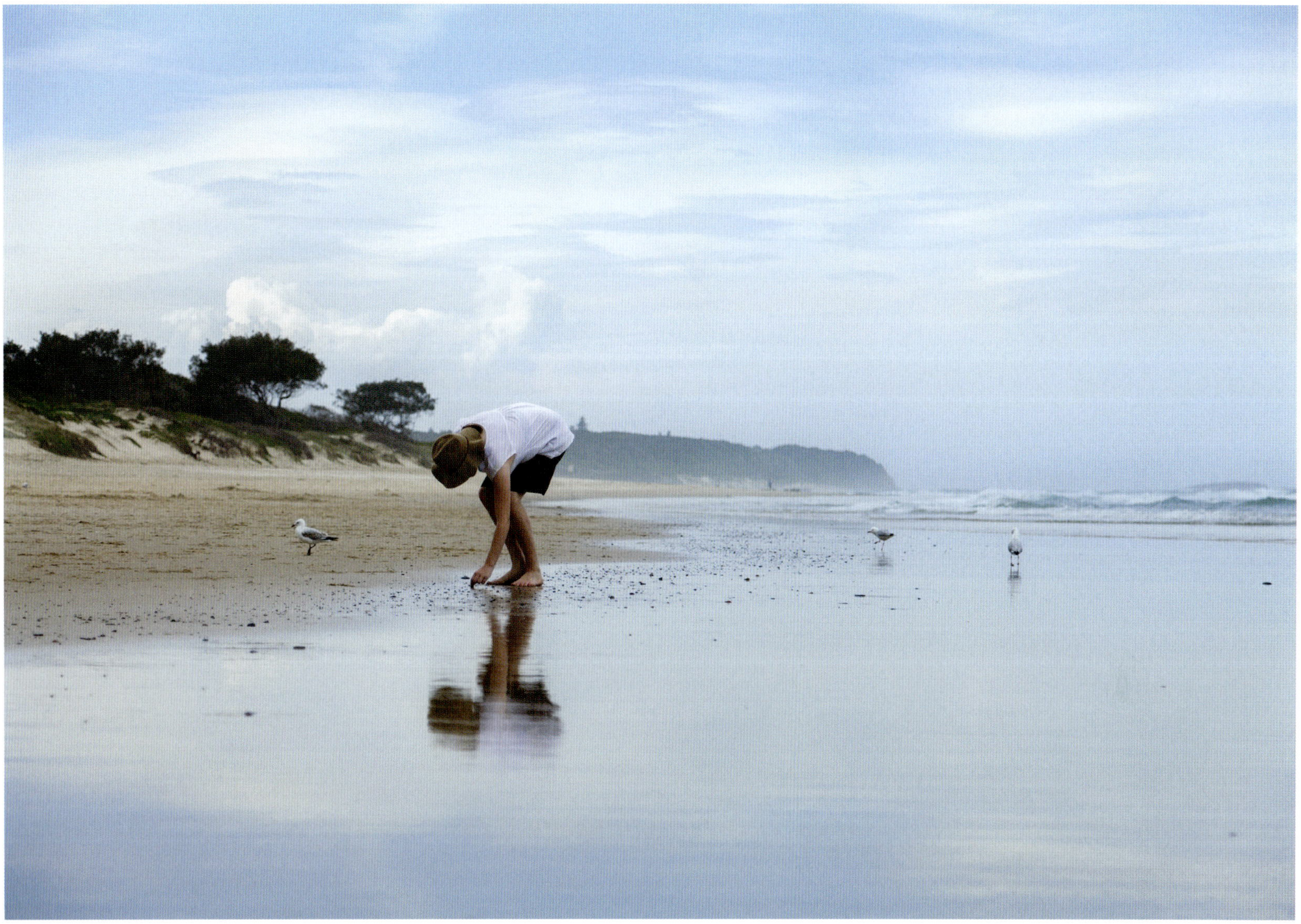

Above, left to right: North Stradbroke Island, Queensland;
Fraser Island, Queensland; Coochiemudlo Island, Queensland
Following spread: Soldiers Point, New South Wales

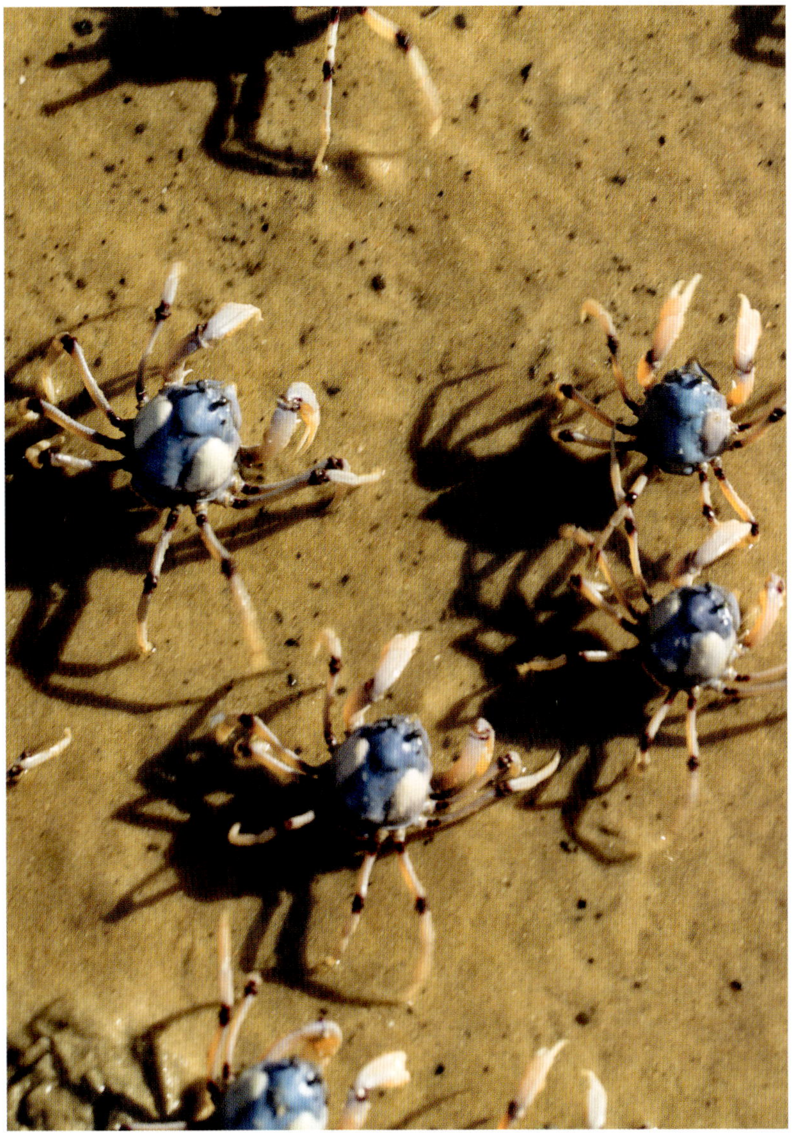

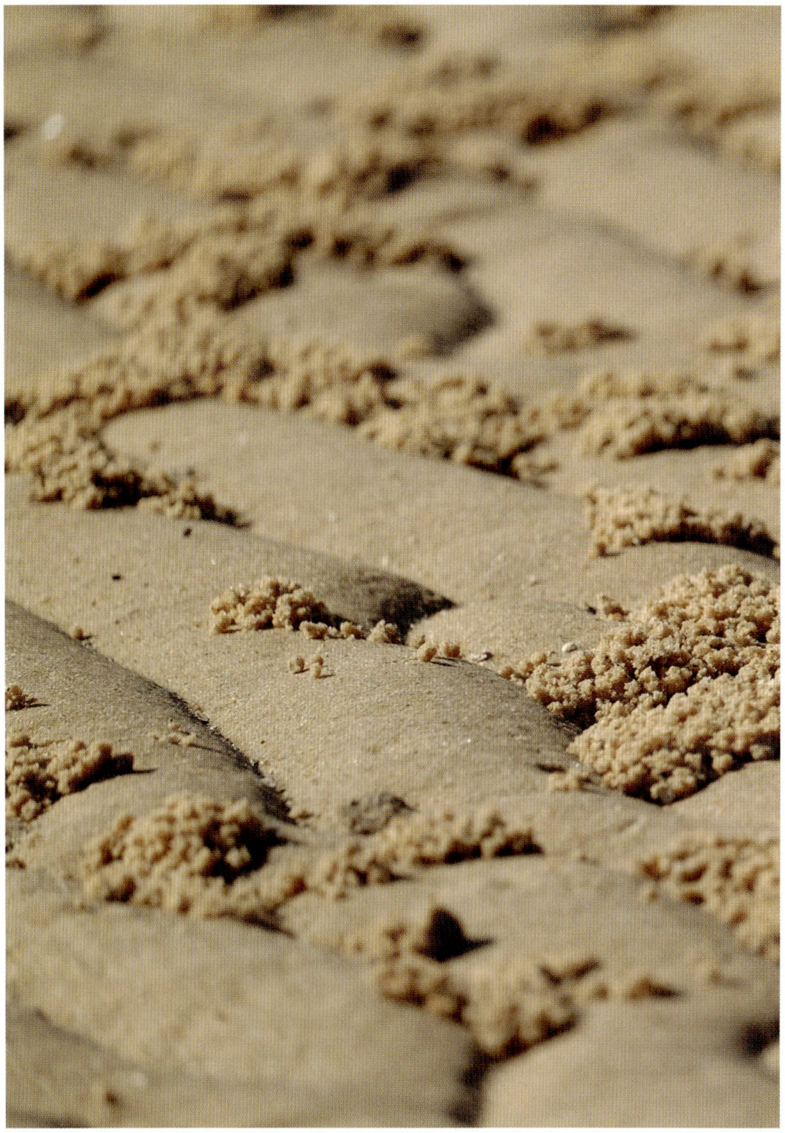

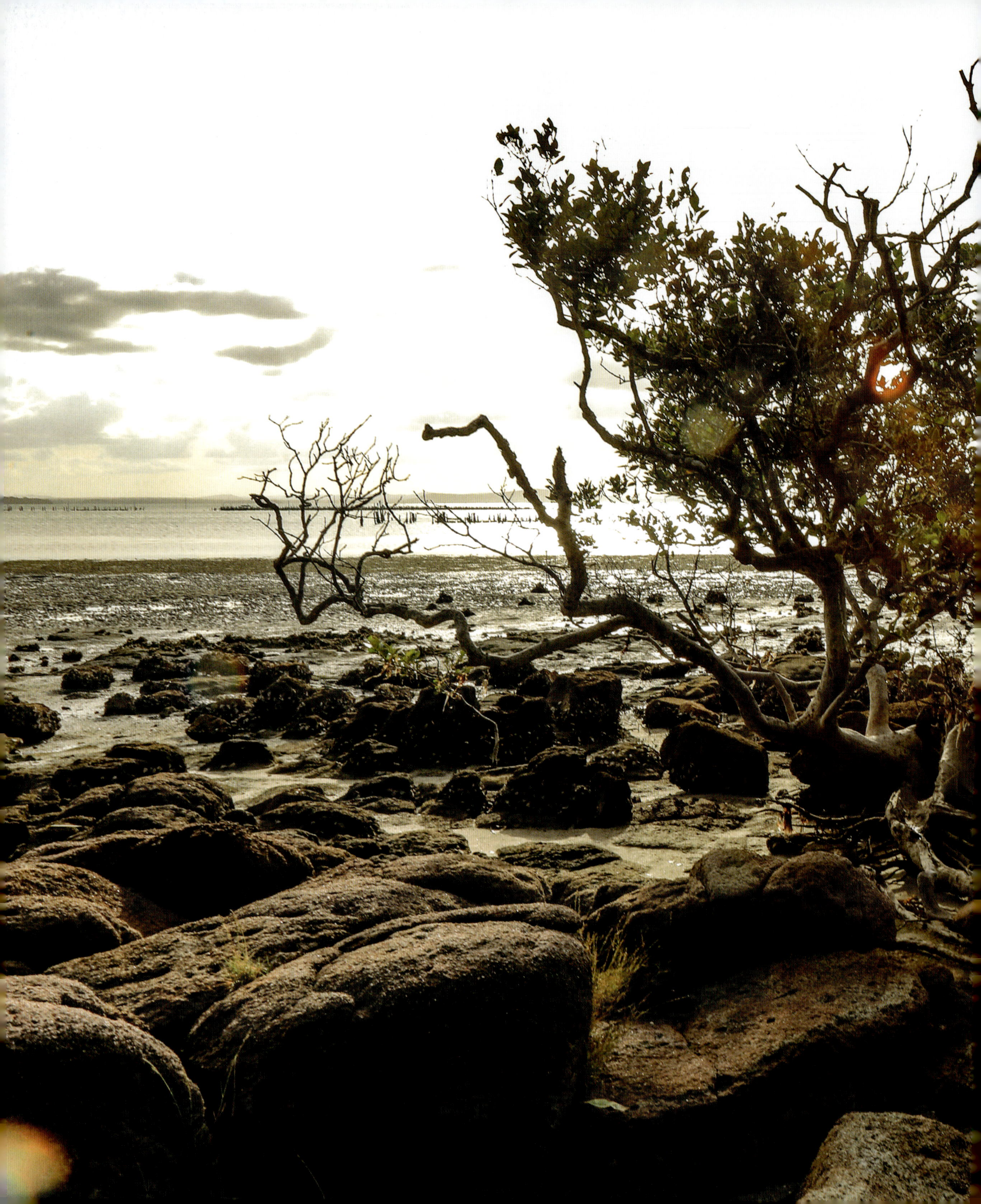

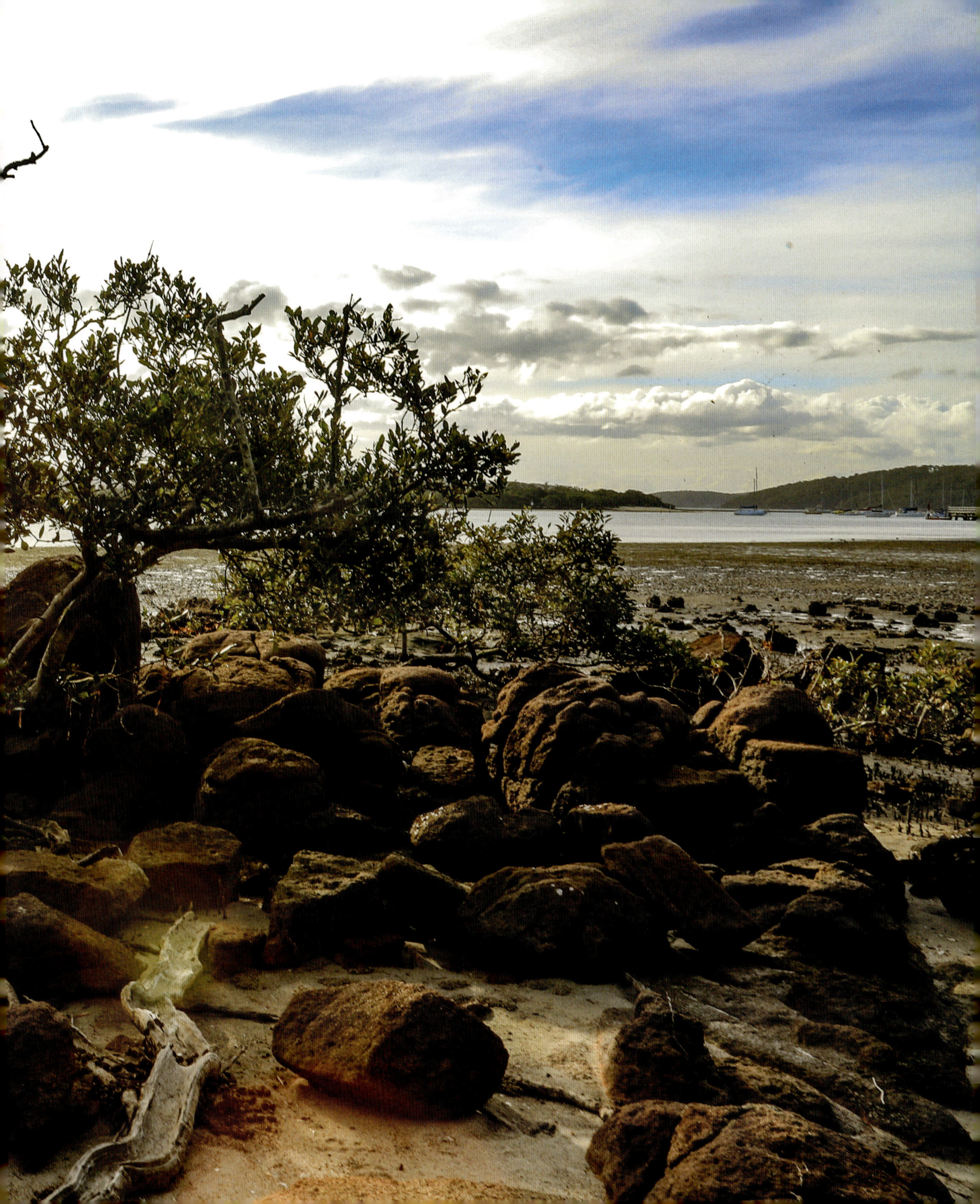

Left to right: Port Fairy, Victoria; Coolangatta, Queensland;
Point Arkwright, Queensland; Fitzgerald River National Park, Western Australia

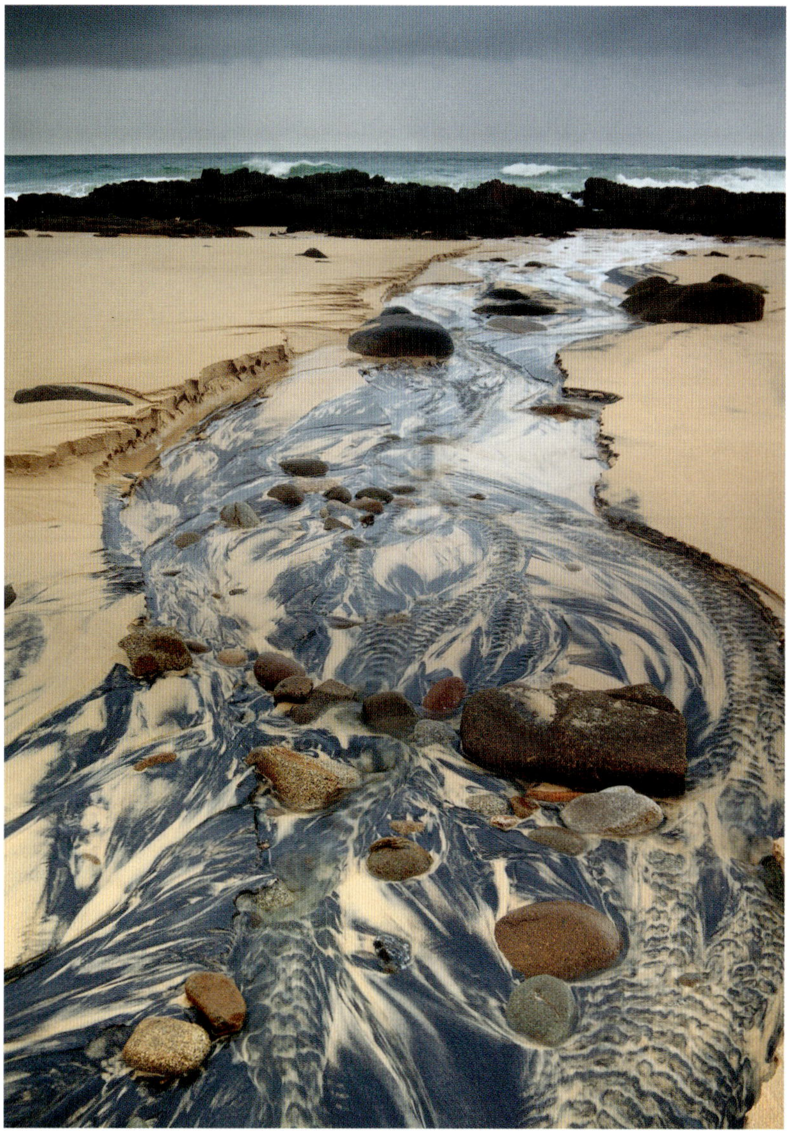

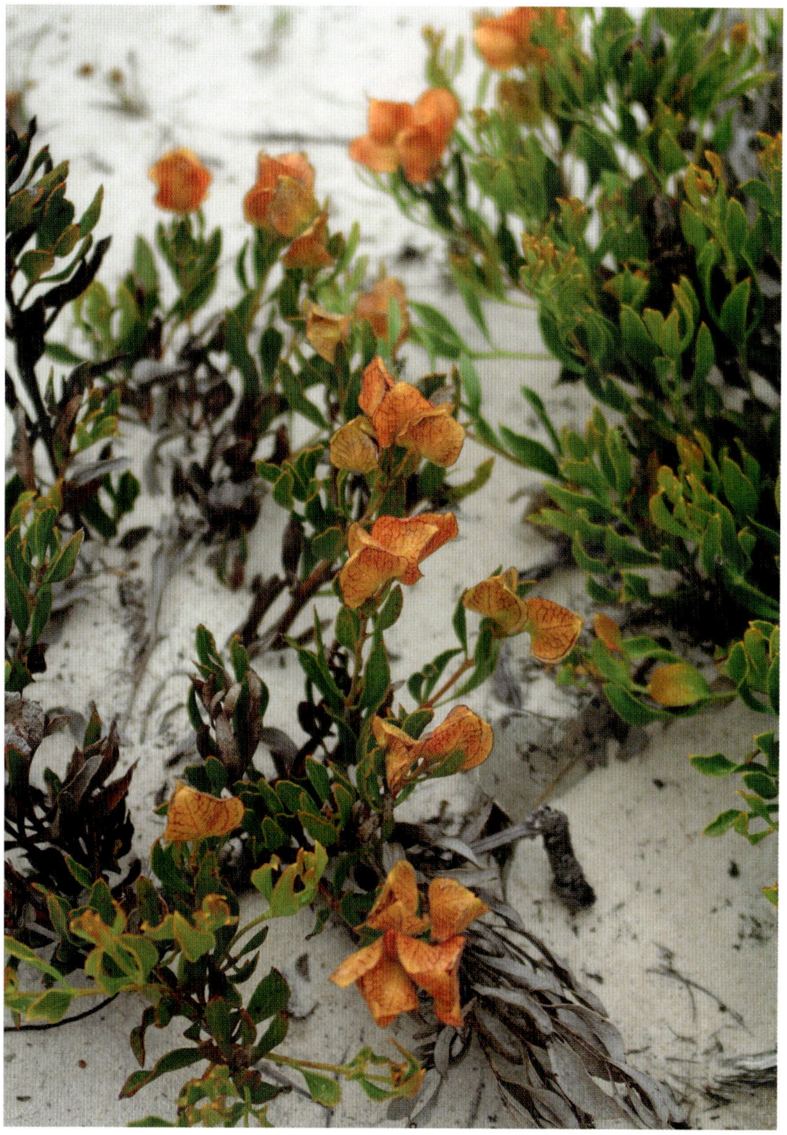

Above and right: Sorrento, Western Australia

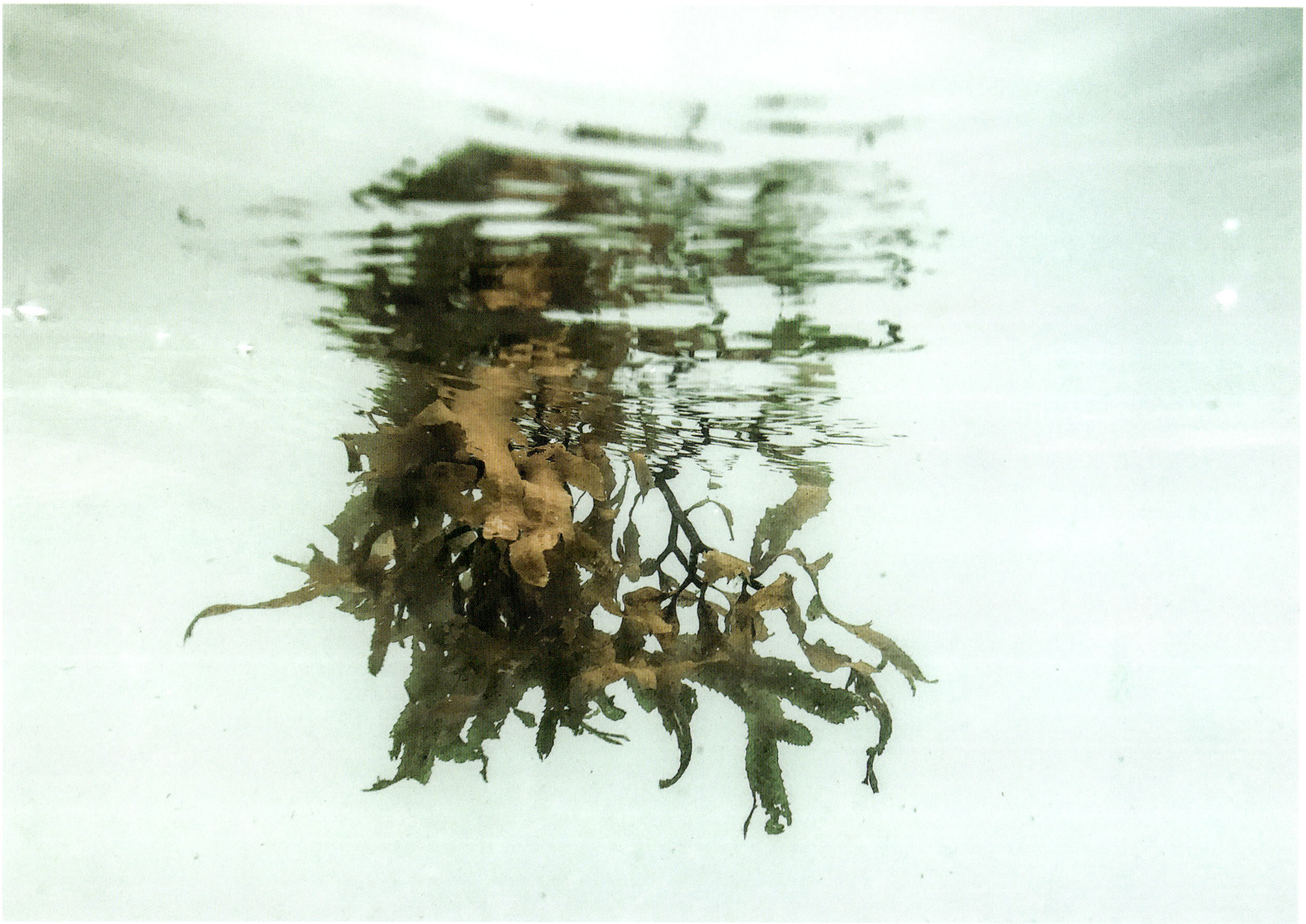

Life at the Edge

Coles Bay, Tasmania

Discover

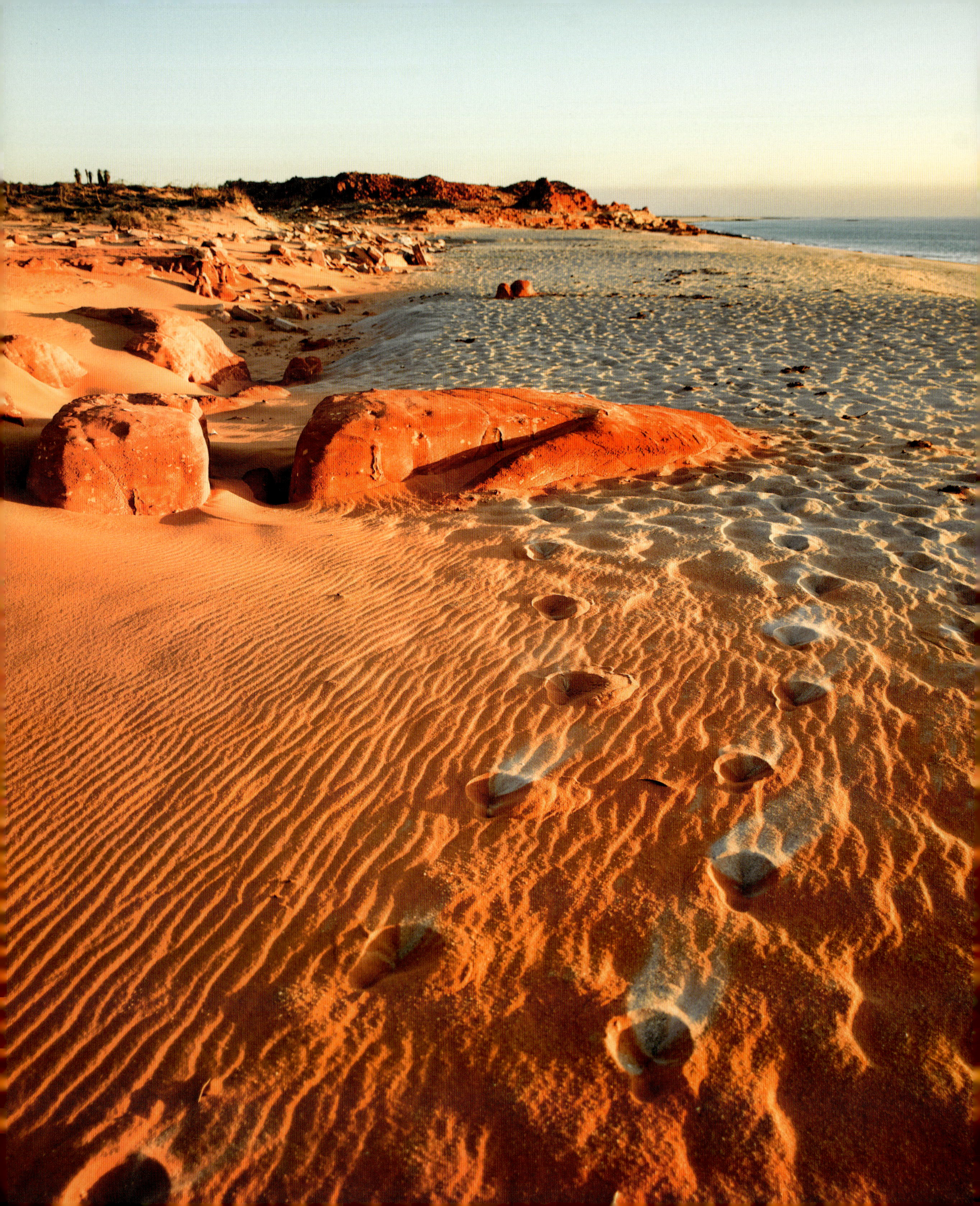

Discover 135

Left: Cape Leveque, Western Australia
Above: Melbourne, Victoria

Above and right: Bunbury, Western Australia

Discover

Life at the Edge

Above, left to right: Caves Beach, New South Wales; Yamba, New South Wales;
Pearl Beach, New South Wales; Bicheno, Tasmania
Following spread: Binalong Bay, Tasmania

Discover

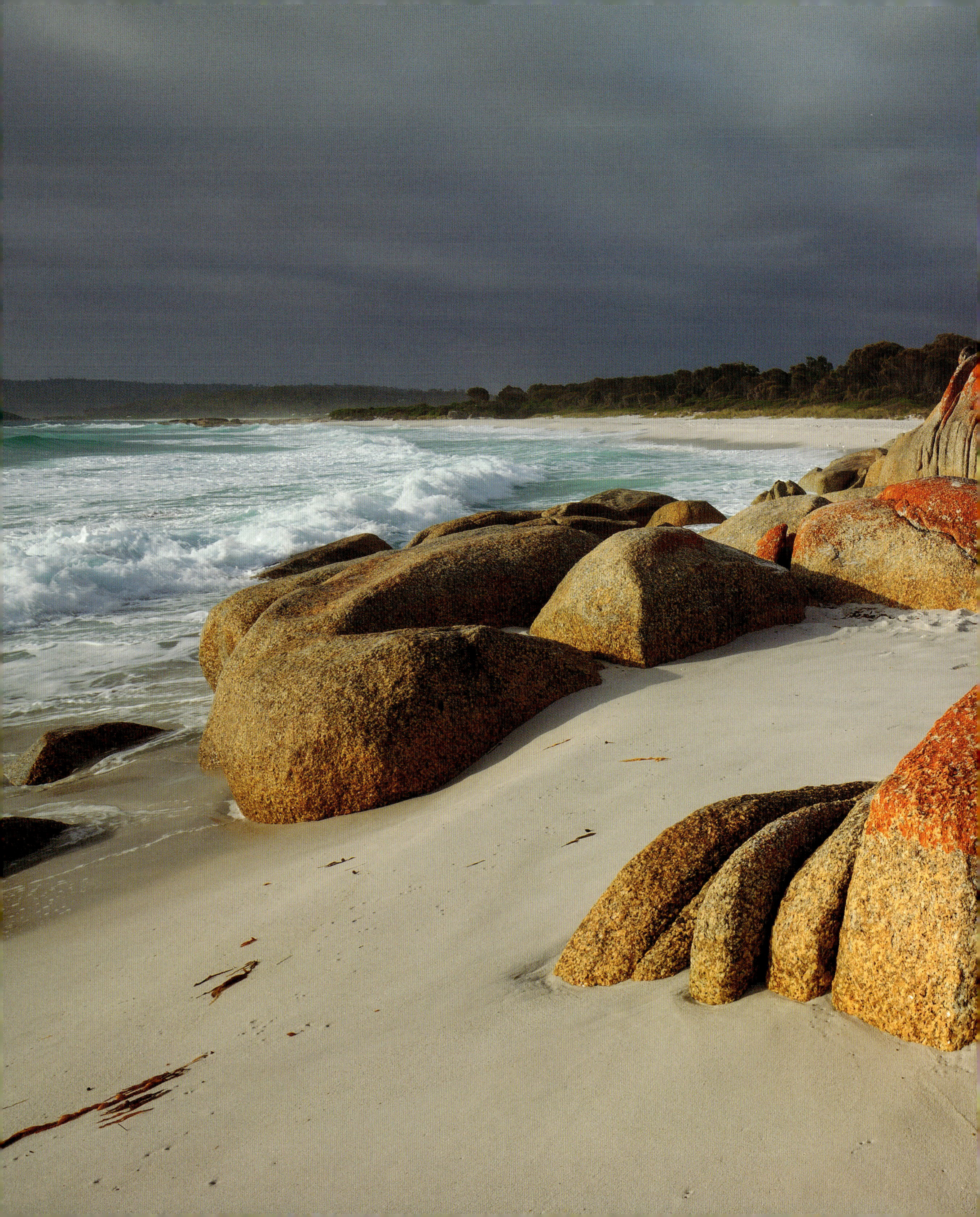

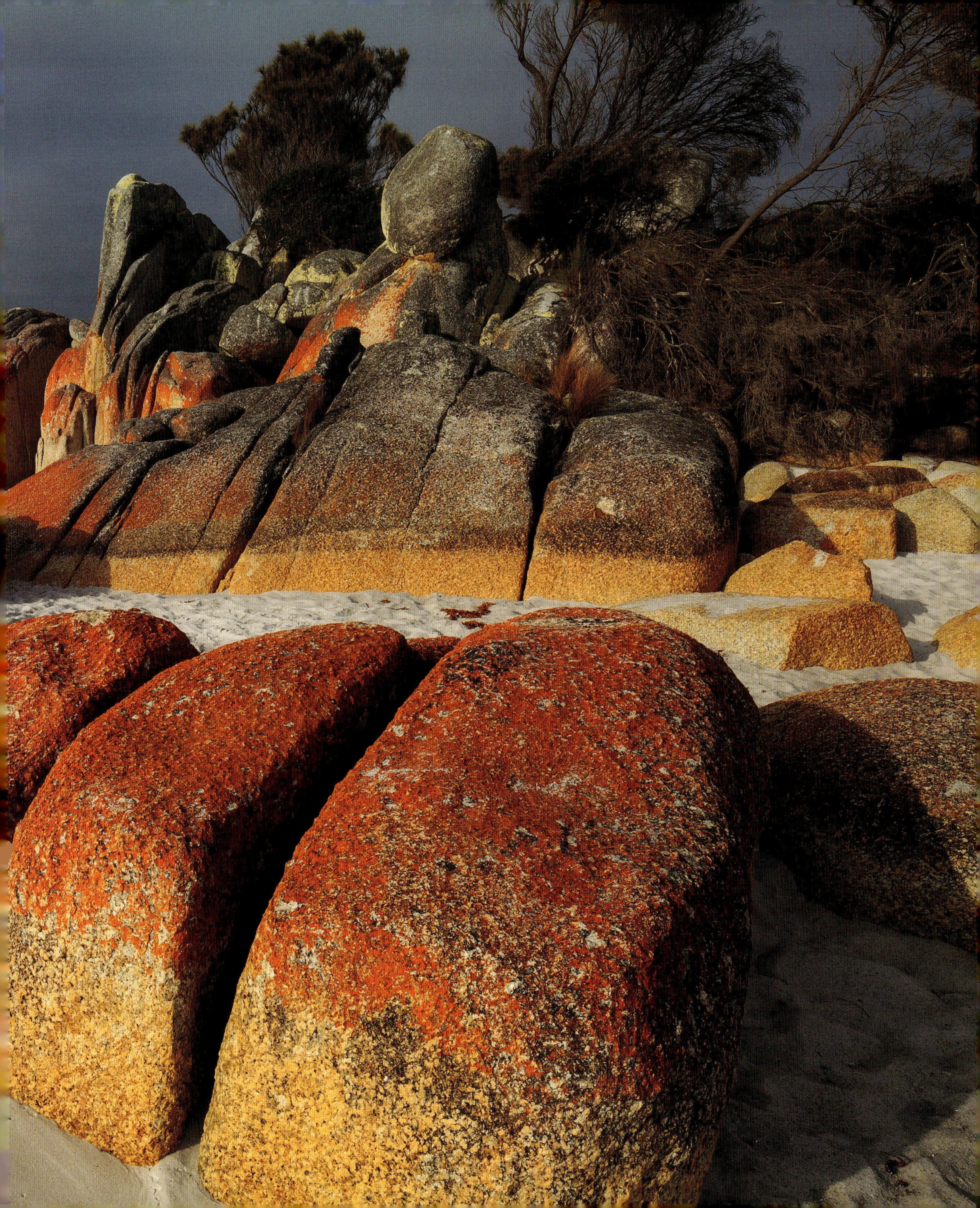

Life at the Edge

Above: Woorim, Queensland
Right: Eaglehawk Neck, Tasmania

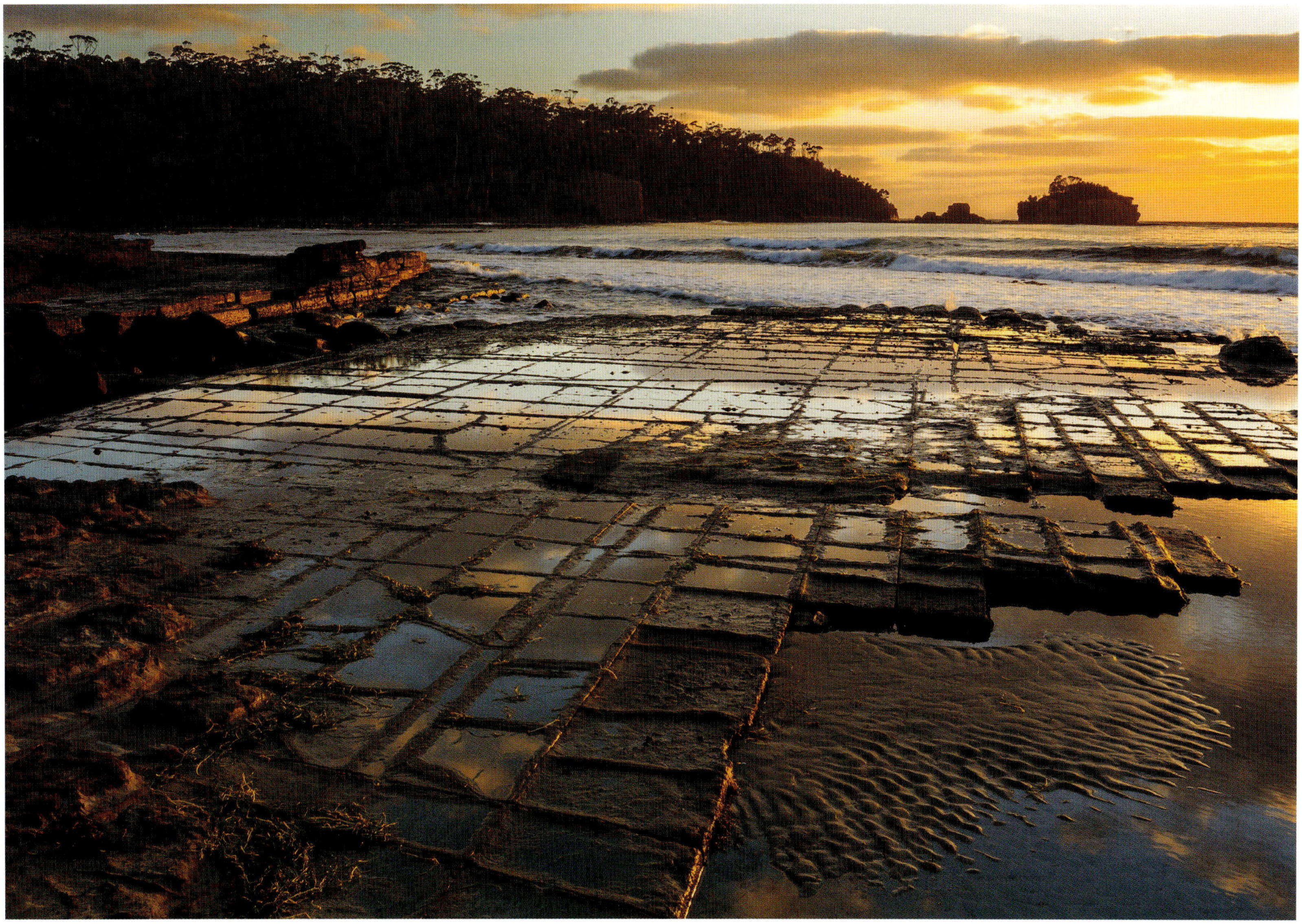

Above, left to right: Currimundi, Queensland; Shelly Beach, Queensland
Right: Aireys Inlet, Victoria

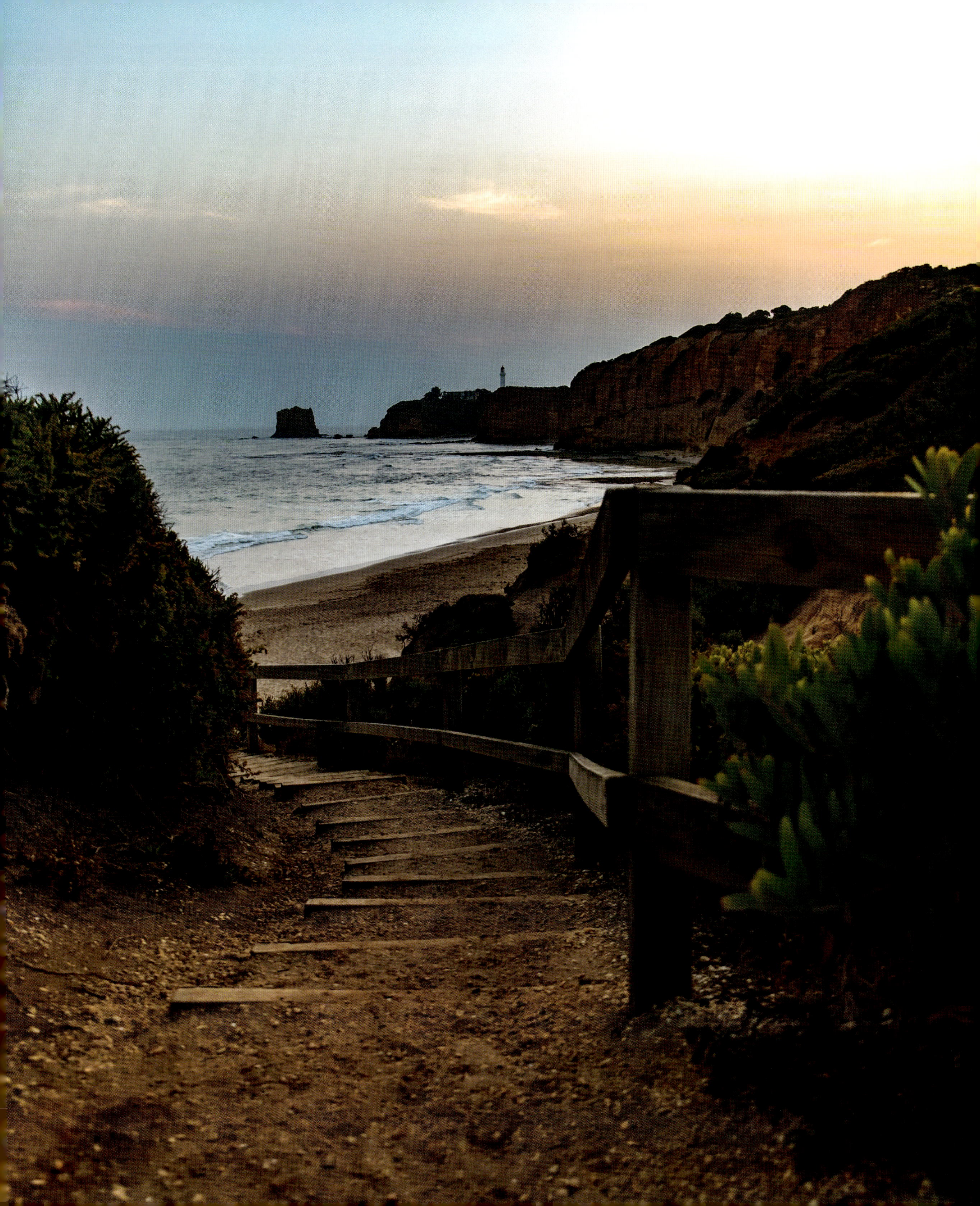

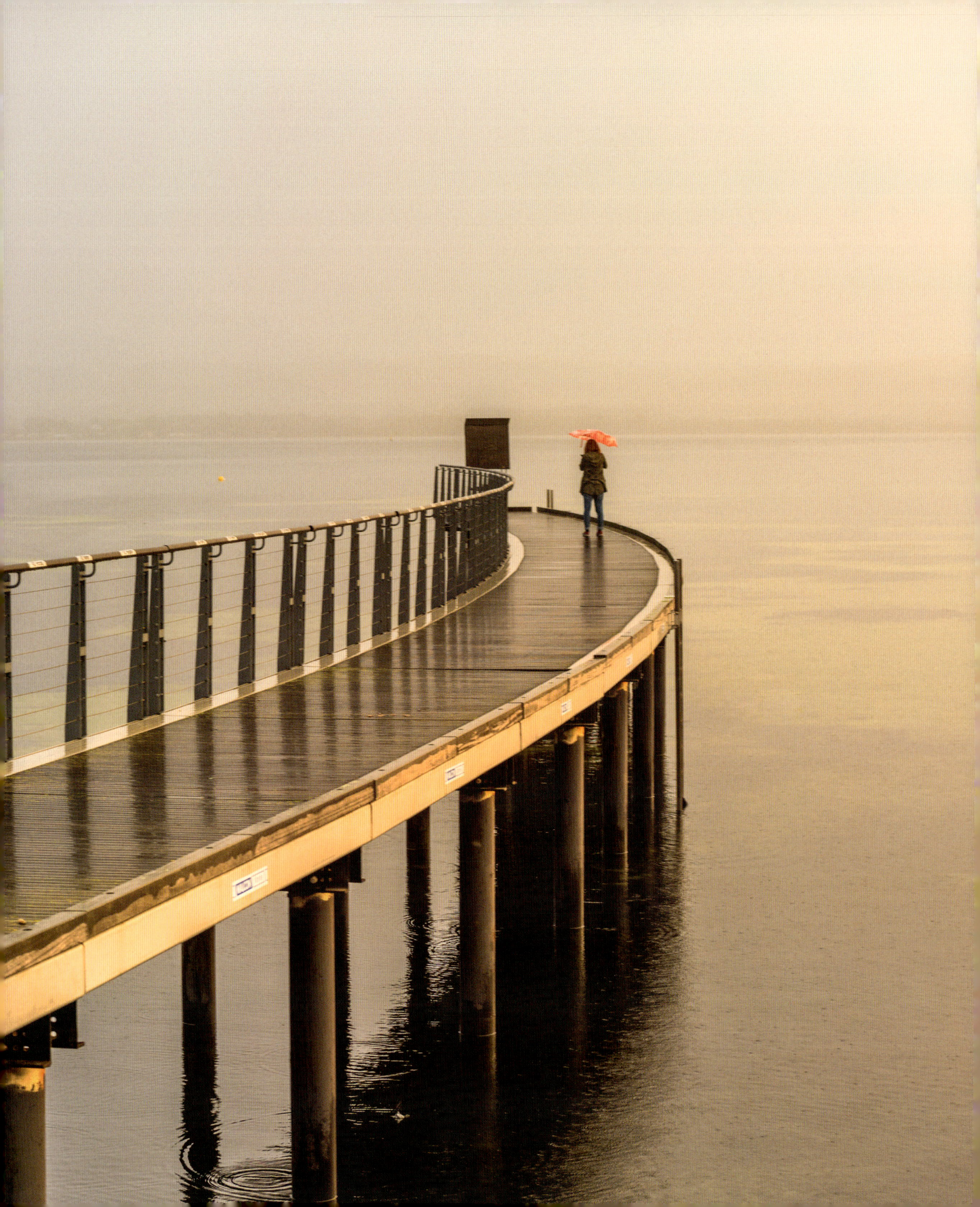

Discover 147

Left: Albany, Western Australia
Above: Yelarbon, Queensland

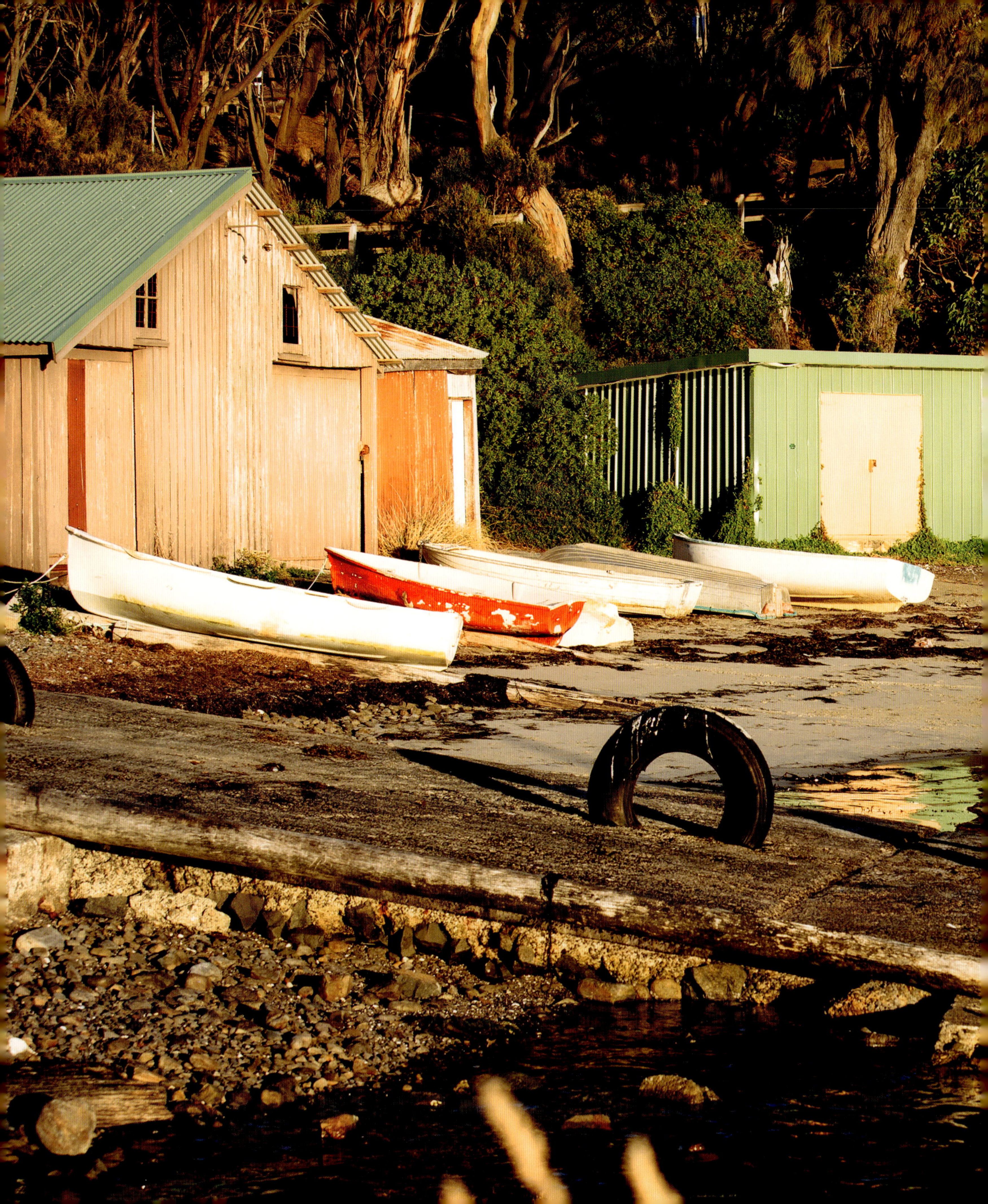

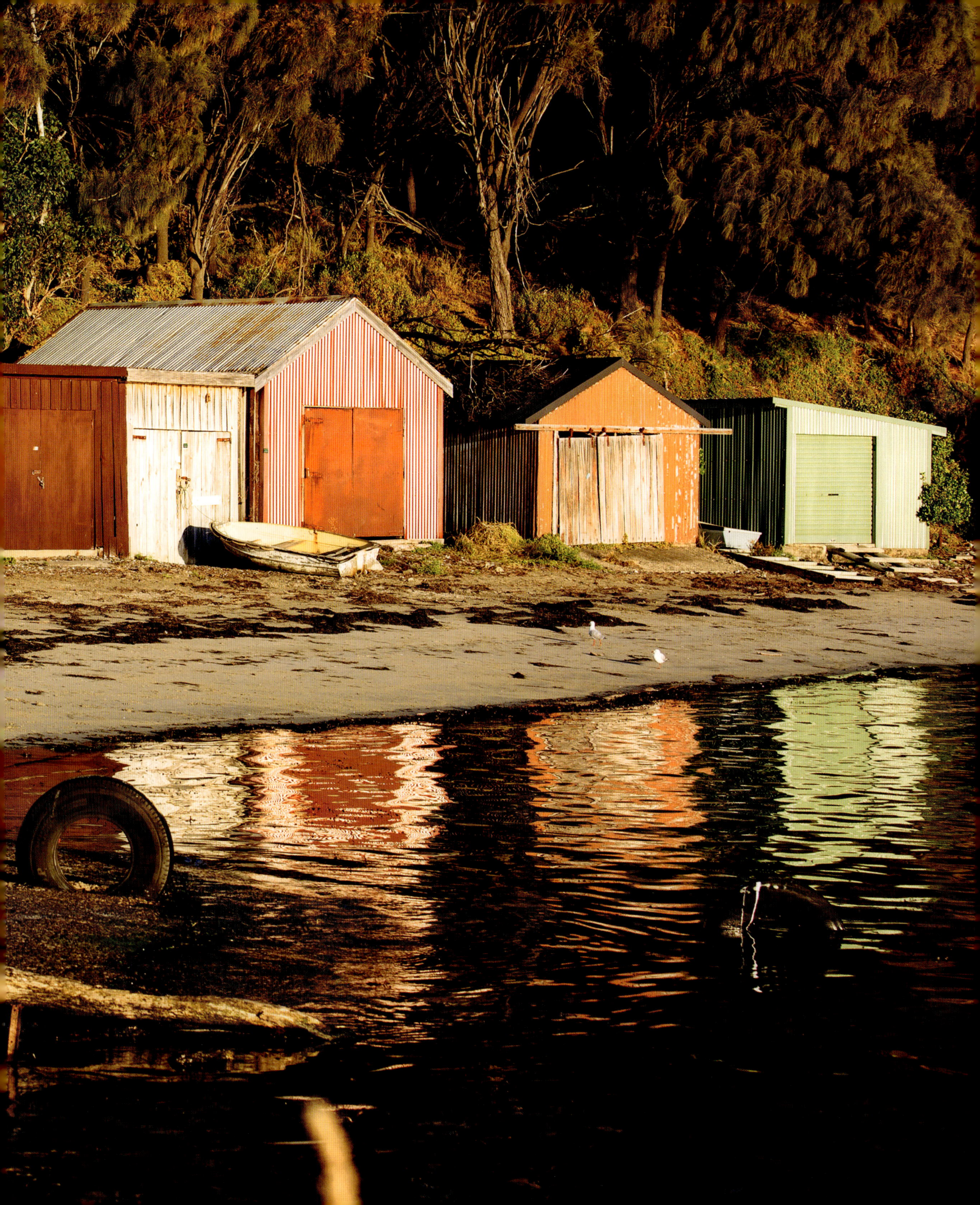

Previous spread: Eaglehawk Neck, Tasmania
Above: Tasman National Park, Tasmania

So, why do we love water?

Whether we realise it or not, we are all influenced by our surroundings, and different environments can have a profound effect on how we feel. For many of us, spending time in unthreatening natural environments has a much more positive effect on our physiological and psychological health than built settings:[1] we often intuitively respond to the stress in our lives by seeking out natural environments, especially those that contain water, such as rivers, lakes and the coast.[2] This is because we perceive aquatic environments to be particularly restorative: they create strong positive reactions that improve our mood and promote recovery from stress and mental fatigue.[3]

Of the many theories and approaches proposed to explain why we are drawn to and gain physiological and psychological benefits from natural environments, two of the most dominant are the Stress Recovery Theory[4] and the Attention Restoration Theory.[5]

The Stress Recovery Theory proposes that, during our evolution, humans developed immediate and involuntary emotional and physiological responses to aspects of natural environments. When faced with an acutely stressful situation, the body's sympathetic nervous system triggers a fight-or-flight response, which mobilises the body for action: our breathing rate increases, the heart beats faster, digestion decreases, and glucose is released from the liver for energy. Activating these bodily systems requires energy and is therefore physically exhausting. Although the fight-or-flight response evolved to enable humans to swiftly respond to danger, elements of city living (e.g. overcrowding, loud noises) and everyday life (e.g. the daily commute, work pressure) can also induce this acute stress response. Repeated activation of this response can negatively impact physical and mental health, and such chronic stress may result in high blood pressure, poor sleep, depression and anxiety. However, just as the human body instinctively reacts to negative stimuli, it equally responds to positive stimuli in the natural environment, such as water.[6] In this instance, the parasympathetic nervous system stimulates the body to 'rest and digest': breathing slows, heart rate decreases, digestion increases, and the body's energy supplies are maintained – the body is restored to a state of calm. Therefore, natural settings, such as forests, mountains, lakes and the coast, can promote these more positive emotions and revitalise energy levels by providing a valuable 'breather' from our stresses.

The Attention Restoration Theory focuses on the restoration of 'directed attention', which is when a certain task requires effort and does not automatically attract one's attention.[7] Prolonged or intense periods of concentration can be mentally exhausting and, as we struggle to focus, we become easily distracted, irritable and impatient; before long, we need to take a break. This theory proposes that our mental fatigue could be reduced by spending time in, or even simply viewing, a restorative environment.[8] As we find nature intrinsically fascinating, viewing natural environments takes no effort and this undemanding attention allows our brains to rest and mentally recover.

Natural environments containing water are especially captivating, engaging all of our senses. Watching a raging river, hearing a thundering waterfall, running our hands through a cool stream, licking salt from our skin and smelling the ocean are all sensory experiences that can transform our moods and stir our emotions.

As vision is our most dominant sense, colour is an important part of our sensory experience and, while water is naturally clear, we associate water most positively with shades of blue: the turquoise of tropical seas to the sapphire blue of the ocean depths. Potentially, we are intuitively drawn to the colour blue as we associate it with fresh water and food.[9] However, we also associate blue with feelings of calm, tranquillity and healing, so we may be drawn to water as we instinctively find it soothing and restorative.[10]

The interplay between water and light can also capture one's attention, creating patterns that we find fascinating. One type of pattern is a fractal – a term first used in 1975 by mathematician Benoît Mandelbrot – which occurs when a pattern repeats itself as it gets larger or smaller.[11] Although some fractals are 'exact', meaning the pattern repeats itself exactly, the fractals found in nature are more random: a tree trunk dividing into smaller branches, a river delta, snowflakes, ocean waves, lightning. Studies have found that viewing the type of fractal pattern experienced in nature can induce 'alpha responses' in the brain, indicative of a relaxed, yet awake, state.[12] This is why watching waves break on the shore, for instance, can be relaxing, calming and, for some, can 'wash away' upsetting emotions.[13]

Comparatively, less research has focused on nature experiences with our other senses, despite their undoubted evolutionary importance for our survival.[14] Sound, however, appears to have received more attention than touch, taste and smell, with several studies highlighting our preference for sounds of nature, such as water, wind and birdsong, over anthropogenic sounds, such as traffic noise.[15] Water arguably has as many sounds as it has colours: a gurgling brook, a tropical rainstorm, the sea washing across and through pebbles, or waves crashing on the shore. These sounds can create a range of feelings and emotions: they can exhilarate and excite, rejuvenate and energise, or relax and calm. The sound of water can be therapeutic and stress-relieving.

While our various sensory experiences in nature are not equally represented in research, there does appear to be an increasing awareness of and drive to explore our other senses like smell, taste and touch.[16] This further work may be especially important considering that we can, quite literally, immerse ourselves in water: swimming and bathing, for instance, create an altogether different way to experience the natural world that is not possible on land.[17]

Water can mean different things to different people: it is a medium in which to relax, reflect, socialise and achieve. Water captivates, calms, invigorates and excites us. This is why we love it.

Dr Deborah Cracknell

Contributors

DR DEBORAH CRACKNELL
Dr Deborah Cracknell is a multidisciplinary researcher with a particular interest in the relationship between natural environments and human health and wellbeing. With a background in marine biology, she undertook a PhD in environmental psychology to study how viewing marine biodiversity influenced people's physiological and psychological health and wellbeing. Her book, *By the Sea: The therapeutic benefits of being in, on and by the water*, aims to impart some of her research, and that of many others, to a wider audience. Deborah also has a keen interest in sustainability issues and is currently working on two sustainability-related projects, including one looking at ways to reduce plastic pollution in the marine environment.

AMY LIPTROT
Amy Liptrot grew up on a sheep farm in the Orkney islands, Scotland. Her bestselling memoir, *The Outrun* won the Wainwright Prize for nature writing and the PEN Ackerely Prize for memoir. It has been translated into 16 languages. She is a lifelong diarist and outdoor swimmer. She lives in Yorkshire with her partner and two young children and her second book *The Instant* will be published in the UK in 2022.

JOCK SERONG
Jock Serong is the author of five novels and has been a criminal lawyer, a senior writer for *Surfing World* magazine and the founding editor of *Great Ocean Quarterly*. Jock has completed a PhD in Creative Writing at La Trobe University. His freelance work is published in *The Guardian*, *The Monthly*, *The Big Issue*, *Tracks*, *The Surfer's Journal*, the *Sydney Morning Herald*, the *Australian Financial Review* and many more outlets. Since leaving legal practice, he has taught law at Deakin University and still teaches writing through festivals and writers' organisations. His latest novel is *The Burning Island*.

KELLIE BALDWIN
Unique experiences are a constant theme in Kellie Baldwin's life. Kellie lives for outdoor adventures and spent her childhood getting dusty and sandy in remote Australian destinations off the beaten track. There began her love affair with the ocean, travel and all things visual. Kellie lives in the coastal burbs of WA with her hubby, son and dog. You'll find her there chasing a wave or that elusive 'light'.
@kelonthecoast.folio

CHARLIE BLACKER
Charlie Blacker is a passionate landscape, nature and adventure photographer. He lives and works out of a self-built camper van, travelling and exploring Australia. If he doesn't have a camera in his hand, you'll find him in the surf or fixing his van.

BEN BLANCHE
Ben Blanche is an adventurous photographer with an affinity for nature and the outdoors. He loves challenges and solving problems in a creative way. Ben was named the Australian Geographic Nature Photographer of the Year 2020.
benblanche.com

GARY CHAPMAN
Gary Chapman was hooked on photography at the age of 14, when he learned to use an old Kodak 126. He made a drastic career change, as his interest in his hobby rapidly overtook his career aspirations. For Gary, there is no greater thrill than watching the light change and transform a landscape.
photographers.com.au/garychapman

CYNTHIA CHEW
Cynthia Chew loves to eat, travel, take pictures and tell stories.

KALIE CHRISTIAN
Originally from the US, Kalie Christian currently lives just outside of Melbourne, VIC. She lives to travel and loves capturing the Australian landscape from an 'outsiders' perspective.
@kalielarae

LOUISE DENTON
Primarily a landscape and nature photographer in the Top End of Australia, Louise Denton is based in Darwin, NT. She travels around the iconic areas of Kakadu, Litchfield and Katherine.
louisedenton.com

CHERI DESAILLY
Cheri Desailly combines her passion for photography with a love of the environment and wildlife.
cheridesailly.com

ROSALIE DIBBEN
Living in a rural area and travelling into pastoral and semi-remote areas allows Rosalie Dibben to see some of the less common parts of this amazing country. Picking up a camera always helps her relax, and she loves capturing the moments and sights that catch her eye anywhere she goes.

CAROL DUNCAN
A self-confessed photography junkie, Carol Duncan is in love with where she lives in Albany, WA. Never without her camera, she loves sharing her view of the world through a passion for landscape and creative fine art photography.
carolduncanphotography.com.au

PAIDI FLYNN
Paidi Flynn is a landscape photographer from Teesdale, VIC. For as long as he can remember, he has had a passion for capturing images of the natural world.
paidiflynn.com

KATE GARCIA
Candid moments, innocent kids and eyes with stories to tell inspire Kate Garcia's photography.

LACHLAN GARDINER
Lachlan Gardiner is driven by a passion to see and experience new places, meet new people and live a life full of adventure. As a photographer, he enjoys spending time in the outdoors and capturing the amazing landscapes that exist in this world. He loves to travel and explore his home country of Australia, experiencing the vast and diverse topography that makes up this beautiful land.
lachlangardiner.com

NICHOLAS GOLDHURST
An avid off-track traveller living in Darwin, NT, Nicholas Goldhurst carries his camera wherever he goes.
ngphotographics.com

JJ HALANS
JJ Halans is a Sydney-based photographer.
halansphotography.com

JON HARRIS
Jon Harris caught the photography bug while working for Parks Australia. In 2014 he took a leap of faith, quitting his job to pursue photography full time and moving to Gerringong, an incredibly photogenic part of the NSW South Coast.
jonharris.photography

NICOLE HASTINGS
Nicole Hastings is a child of the 80s, lover of retro and vintage, mother and photographer.
nicolehastings.com

MICHAEL HERITAGE
Michael Heritage's passion for travel and adventure has led him to spend a number of years island hopping around the world with an occasional city stop over for an urban fix and good coffee. He is currently based on the coast in WA.
michael-heritage.com

JUSTIN HEVEY
Justin Hevey is an independent photographer/designer living in Sydney, NSW, with his young family and a great collection of vintage film cameras.
idocumentspace.com

CRAIG HOLLOWAY
After working as a commercial photographer in Ballarat, VIC, for eight years, Craig Holloway and his partner, Paula, decided to travel around the country. Craig's 'Abandoned Places' photographs document the forgotten and forlorn.
craighollowayphotographer.com

BRAYDEN HOWIE
Brayden Howie loves creating images of amazing people and fabulous places – the further off the beaten track, the better. He has had the privilege of telling stories from some of the most formidable locations in the planet: from North Korea and Myanmar to remote Mongolia and rural Timor-Leste, from the Blue Mountains National Park to his very own backyard.
@noborders.photography

SAM IRWIN
Sam Irwin first picked up a film camera at the age of 10, 25 years later he is still taking photos and making videos.
samirwin.com

KATHRYN JEWKES
Located on the Central Coast of NSW, Kathryn Jewkes is a photographer who loves to capture everyday moments with her daughters. She loves sunny days and spending time with her family at the beach or exploring the local national parks.

BIANCA LAI
Influenced by her father's photography, Bianca Lai developed an early interest in cameras. This grew into a passion for capturing the natural wonders she finds on her travels.
@beeandcar

MARTIN LAURICELLA
Martin Lauricella loves the landscape and diverse fauna and flora of Australia. He explores his surroundings with photography – from day to night, huge vistas to macros, the everyday to the extraordinary.

BILLIE LEATHAM
Billie Leatham is a mother, wife and photographer living and working in rural VIC. Raising her family on the land and being surrounded by beauty and wonder provides daily inspiration.
@billiemaephotography

JESS LIVINGSTONE
Jess Livingstone is a landscape architect and mum with a keen interest in photography. She uses her camera to capture what she loves about the Australian landscape – its textures, colours, details and scale.

ANGELA LUMSDEN
Angela Lumsden is a documentary photographer located near the beach in WA and is inspired to capture the beauty in everyday life and preserve memories of these fleeting years – gorgeous light, real people, authentic moments and breathtaking surroundings.
angelalumsden.com

DANIEL MADDOCK
Daniel Maddock's idea of perfection is an all-day hike accompanied by his fifty-year-old Hasselblad loaded with Kodak Portra 400 film stock, followed by a quiet night with a novel. Capturing the natural beauty of this wonderful country in perfect light with simple old-fashioned celluloid film is how he likes to take a picture.

ARNI MANGAHAS
A long-time love of landscape photography and a new-found love of photographing humans allows Arni Mangahas to create unique compositions in which the two styles meet halfway.

ANDREW MCINNES
Andrew McInnes is a husband, dad and photographer based in South East QLD.
andrewmcinnes.com

JUSTIN MCKINNEY
Photography is Justin McKinney's escape from reality. He is passionate about travel and landscape photography and capturing Australia as he sees it.

MATT MURRAY
Matt Murray loves travelling and exploring new places. Visiting over 30 countries in Europe and Asia has given him a new perspective on the unique beauty of Australia.
@mattloves

JODIE NASH
A theatre nurse for more than a decade, Jodie Nash uses her photography to share the beauty of land, sea and animals.

ROWENA NAYLOR
Rowena Naylor is a professional photographer living a glorious life in country VIC, with a love of capturing everyday life in rural Australia.

SHANE PEDERSEN
Shane Pedersen grew up in QLD but has lived in TAS permanently since 2002, and has had great adventures in its many beautiful natural areas. A love of nature and spectacular wild places is what inspires Shane to go to extraordinary efforts at times to capture just the right image.

ROBERT PORTER
Robert Porter is based in Brisbane, QLD. He has a love of landscape, street and black-and-white photography.
portadown.picfair.com

GARY RADLER
A husband, father, grandfather and lover of photography, Gary Radler works both as a psychologist and a photographer.
garyradler.com

DINITHI RANATHUNGA
Dinithi Ranathunga's photography is about telling a beautiful story through capturing the everyday. She is drawn to creative light and her images are constantly inspired by the golden hour.

JONAH RITCHIE
Jonah Ritchie is a Sydney-based lifestyle photographer with 10+ years of professional experience shooting for a wide range of commercial and editorial clients in Australia and internationally.

CLARE SEIBEL-BARNES
Clare Seibel-Barnes began her career as a photographer capturing small details: things she found in the shed, the yard, her hometown – things close to her heart. As her horizons expanded, Clare found inspiration in Australia's sweeping plains, silvery dew-spangled mornings and afternoons flooded in golden light.
clearlightphotography.com.au

FRANCESCO SOLFRINI
Francesco Solfrini is an Italian-born, Sydney-based photographer fascinated by the ever-changing faces and personalities of people.

RUNE SVENSDEN
Rune Svensden is a Norwegian photographer who has lived in Australia since 2013. Since living in Sydney, NSW, his mission has been to seek out new and fresh angles across the city, harbour and beaches. He enjoys capturing well-known landmarks with his very own twist and style.
@svendsania

CARO TELFER
Caro Telfer is a rural-based, AIPP-accredited professional photographer who is married to a farmer. Her studio is in Darkan, in the Wheatbelt region of WA.
carotelfer.com

LEAH-ANNE THOMPSON
Leah-Anne Thompson's passion for adventure sees her travel in her 4x4 campervan to Australia's wilderness, outback and coast to photograph the landscape and nature she so adores. Her photography is a mix of professional and ad hoc real-life moments.

GILLIAN VANN
Having travelled widely across this great big land, Gillian Vann now calls the glorious Northern Beaches of Sydney, NSW, home.

DAVID VEENTJER
David Veentjer enjoys taking photographs of everyday life in the suburbs of Melbourne, VIC.

CLAUDIA WASKOW
Claudia Waskow began her photography career as a professional real estate photographer and was soon drawn to capturing everything else in order to challenge and hone her skills. She loves how light can be used to change the look and mood in her photography, especially when photographing children and animals at play. 'Photography has taught me to stand still and observe and find joy in the most amazing places and creatures. I love hearing the shutter click and then being able to view the image instantly. It is my ultimate satisfaction to capture the essence of what I love about Australia.'
allpropertyphotography.com

JANE WORNER
Jane Worner started taking photos when she was an aid worker, travelling the world being inspired by people and places. The arrival of twins saw her return to her hometown, Wombat, NSW. She takes photos as often as she can, inspired by our wonderful people and country. As a farmer and passionate plant person, Jane is drawn to rural scenes and plant and garden portraits.

Image Credits

Contents & Introduction

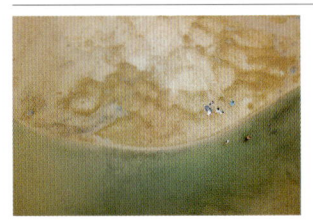

Gary Chapman

Clare Seibel-Barnes

Gary Chapman

Rosalie Dibben

p. 7 — Francesco Solfrini

Play

p. 8 — Kellie Baldwin

p. 10 — Kellie Baldwin

p. 12 — Kellie Baldwin

p. 13 — Brayden Howie

p. 14 — Bianca Lai

p. 15 — Francesco Solfrini

p. 16 — Kellie Baldwin

p. 18 — Arni Mangahas

p. 19 — Bianca Lai

p. 20 — Kathryn Jewkes

p. 21 — David Veentjer

p. 22 — Jonah Ritchie

p. 23 — Rowena Naylor

p. 24 — Kellie Baldwin

p. 26 — Clare Seibel-Barnes

p. 27 — Clare Seibel-Barnes

p. 28 — Caro Telfer

p. 29 — Dinithi Ranathunga

p. 30 — Gary Radler

p. 32 — JJ Halans

p. 34 — Kellie Baldwin

p. 35 — Kellie Baldwin

p. 36 — Justin Hevey

p. 38 — Kellie Baldwin

p. 39 — Matt Murray

Live

p. 40 — Gillian Vann

p. 42 — Lachlan Gardiner

p. 44 — Nicole Hastings

p. 45 — Gary Chapman (left)
Ben Blanche (right)

p. 46 — Cheri Desailly

p. 47 — Daniel Maddock

p. 48 — Jane Worner

p. 49 — Kalie Christian

p. 50 — Matt Murray

P. 52 — Leah-Anne Thompson

p. 54 — Robert Porter

p. 55 — Claudia Waskow (left)
Cheri Desailly (right)

p. 56 — Justin McKinney

p. 57 — Craig Holloway

p. 58 — Gary Chapman (left)
Robert Porter (right)

p. 59 — Gary Chapman

p. 60 — Jon Harris

p. 62 — Rowena Naylor (left)
Jess Livingstone (right)

p. 63 — Andrew McInnes

p. 64 — Paidi Flynn

156

p. 65 — Gary Radler

p. 66 — Shane Pedersen

p. 68 — Craig Holloway

p. 70 — Jodie Nash

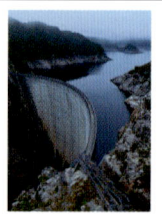

p. 71 — Shane Pedersen

p. 72 — Justin McKinney

Breathe

p. 74 — Rowena Naylor

p. 76 — Andrew McInnes

p. 78 — Martin Lauricella (left)
Jess Livingstone (right)

p. 79 — Craig Holloway (left)
Gary Chapman (right)

p. 80 — Jane Worner

p. 81 — Gary Chapman

p. 82 — Kate Garcia

p. 83 — Leah-Anne Thompson

p. 84 — Sam Irwin

p. 85 — Kellie Baldwin

p. 86 — Louise Denton

p. 88 — Clare Seibel-Barnes

p. 89 — Andrew McInnes

p. 90 — Michael Heritage

p. 91 — Paidi Flynn

p. 92 — Charlie Blacker

p. 94 — Clare Seibel-Barnes

p. 95 — Leah-Anne Thompson

p. 96 — Rosalie Dibben

p. 98 — Nicholas Gouldhurst

p. 99 — Brayden Howie

p. 100 — Cynthia Chew

p. 101 — Caro Telfer

p. 102 — Clare Seibel-Barnes

p. 103 — Francesco Solfrini

p. 104 — Nicholas Gouldhurst

p. 106 — Rosalie Dibben

p. 108 — Gary Chapman

p. 109 — Rosalie Dibben (left)
Jess Livingstone (right)

p. 110 — Caro Telfer

p. 111 — David Veentjer

p. 112 — Kathryn Jewkes

p. 114 — Ben Blanche

Discover

p. 116 — Rune Svensden

p. 118 — Rosalie Dibben

p. 119 — Angela Lumsden

p. 120 — Kellie Baldwin

p. 121 — Billie Leatham

p. 122 — Rosalie Dibben

p. 123 — Clare Seibel-Barnes

p. 124 — Cheri Desailly

p. 125 — Ben Blanche (left)
Matt Murray (right)

p. 126 — Justin McKinney

p. 128 — Rowena Naylor (left)
Andrew McInnes (right)

p. 129 — Gary Chapman (left)
Jess Livingstone (right)

p. 130 — Kellie Baldwin

p. 131 — Kellie Baldwin

p. 132 — Gary Chapman

p. 134 — Craig Holloway

p. 135 — Dinithi Ranathunga

p. 136 — Caro Telfer

p. 137 — Caro Telfer

p. 138 — Clare Seibel-Barnes (left)
Andrew McInnes (right)

p. 139 — Andrew McInnes (left)
Jane Worner (right)

p. 140 — Shane Pedersen

p. 142 — Ben Blanche

p. 143 — Shane Pedersen

p. 144 — Gary Chapman

p. 145 — Jess Livingstone

p. 146 — Carol Duncan

p. 147 — Cheri Desailly

p. 148 — Ben Blanche

p. 150 — Shane Pedersen

Acknowledgements

Many thanks to the photographers who responded from across the country to our call for images of the Australian landscape in all its guises. A special thanks to Claire Bonnor, Director, Austockphoto for all of her help and advice and for making an unwieldy process drama free, and to Caro Telfer for making the trip to Pemberton.

First published in Australia in 2021
by Thames & Hudson Australia Pty Ltd
11 Central Boulevard, Portside Business Park
Port Melbourne, Victoria 3207
ABN: 72 004 751 964

thamesandhudson.com.au

Life at the Edge © Thames & Hudson Australia 2021

The body's ancient memory © Jock Serong 2021
The same sea © Amy Liptrot 2021
So, why do we love water? © Dr Deborah Cracknell 2021
Images © copyright remains with the individual
copyright holders

24 23 22 21   5 4 3 2 1

The moral right of the author has been asserted.

All rights reserved. No part of this publication may be reproduced or transmitted in any form or by any means, electronic or mechanical, including photocopy, recording or any other information storage or retrieval system, without prior permission in writing from the publisher.

Any copy of this book issued by the publisher is sold subject to the condition that it shall not by way of trade or otherwise be lent, resold, hired out or otherwise circulated without the publisher's prior consent in any form of binding or cover other than that in which it is published and without a similar condition including these words being imposed on a subsequent purchaser.

Thames & Hudson Australia wishes to acknowledge that Aboriginal and Torres Strait Islander people are the first storytellers of this nation and the traditional custodians of the land on which we live and work. We acknowledge their continuing culture and pay respect to Elders past, present and future.

ISBN 978-1-760-76120-2

A catalogue record for this book is available from the National Library of Australia

Every effort has been made to trace accurate ownership of copyrighted text and visual materials used in this book. Errors or omissions will be corrected in subsequent editions, provided notification is sent to the publisher.

Front cover: Austinmer, New South Wales; Andrew McInnes
Back cover: Gulf St Vincent, South Australia; Rosalie Dibben
Design: Claire Orrell
Editing: Jo Turner
Printed and bound in China by 1010
Printing International Limited

FSC® is dedicated to the promotion of responsible forest management worldwide. This book is made of material from FSC®-certified forests and other controlled sources.

References for *So, why do we love water?*
by Dr Deborah Cracknell:

1. R S Ulrich et al., 'Stress Recovery During Exposure to Natural and Urban Environments', *Journal of Environmental Psychology*, 11(3), 1991, pp. 201–30.
2. R S Ulrich et al., 'Aesthetic and Affective Response to Natural Environment', in I Altman & J F Wohlwill (eds), *Behaviour and the Natural Environment*, Plenum, New York, 1983, pp. 85–125.
   R S Ulrich et al., 'Stress Recovery During Exposure to Natural and Urban Environments', pp. 201–30.
3. S L Bell et al., 'Seeking Everyday Wellbeing: The Coast as a Therapeutic Landscape', *Social Science & Medicine*, 142, 2015, pp. 56–67.
   M White et al., 'Blue Space: The Importance of Water for Preference, Affect, and Restorativeness Ratings of Natural and Built Scenes', *Journal of Environmental Psychology*, 30(4), 2010, pp. 482–93.
   M White et al., 'Feelings of Restoration from Recent Nature Visits', *Journal of Environmental Psychology*, 35, 2013, pp. 40–51.
4. R S Ulrich, 'Biophilia, Biophobia and Natural Landscapes', in S Kellert & E O Wilson (eds), *The Biophilia Hypothesis*, Island Press, Washington DC, 1993, pp. 73–137.
   R S Ulrich et al., 'Stress Recovery During Exposure to Natural and Urban Environments', pp. 201–30.
5. R Kaplan & S Kaplan, *The Experience of Nature: A Psychological Perspective*, Cambridge University Press, New York, 1989.
6. R S Ulrich, 'Natural Versus Urban Scenes: Some Psychophysiological Effects', *Environment and Behavior*, 13(5), 1981, pp. 523–56.
   R S Ulrich et al., 'Stress Recovery During Exposure to Natural and Urban Environments', pp. 201–30.
7. R Kaplan & S Kaplan.
8. R Kaplan & S Kaplan.
9. M P White et al., 'Do Preferences for Waterscapes Persist in Inclement Weather and Extend to Sub-Aquatic Scenes?', *Landscape Research*, 39(4), 2014, pp. 339–58.
10. Z O'Connor, 'Colour Psychology and Colour Therapy: Caveat Emptor', *Color Research and Application*, 36(3), 2011, pp. 229–34.
11. K Gillis & B Gatersleben, 'A Review of Psychological Literature on the Health and Wellbeing Benefits of Biophilic Design', *Buildings*, 5, 2015, pp. 948–63.
12. C Hägerhäll et al., 'Human Physiological Benefits of Viewing Nature: EEG Responses to Exact and Statistical Fractal Patterns', *Nonlinear Dynamics, Psychology, and Life Sciences*, 19(1), 2015, pp. 1–12.
13. S L Bell et al., pp. 56–67.
14. L S Franco et al., 'A Review of the Benefits of Nature Experiences: More Than Meets the Eye', *International Journal of Environmental Research and Public Health*, 14(8), 2017, p. 864.
15. L S Franco et al., p. 864.
16. L S Franco et al., p. 864.
17. K Rew, *Wild Swim: River, Lake, Lido and Sea: The Best Places to Swim Outdoors in Britain*, Guardian Books, London, 2008.